Teaching Citizenship in the Secondary School

James Arthur and Daniel Wright

David Fulton Publishers

London

David Fulton Publishers Ltd
Ormond House, 26–27 Boswell Street, London WC1N 3JZ

www.fultonpublishers.co.uk

First published in Great Britain by David Fulton Publishers 2001

Note: The rights of James Arthur and Daniel Wright to be identified as the authors of this work has been asserted by them in accordance with the Copyright, Designs and Patents Act 1988.

Copyright © James Arthur and Daniel Wright   2001

British Library Cataloguing in Publication Data
A catalogue record for this book is available from the British Library.

ISBN 1–85346–744–8

Typeset by Book Production Services, London
Printed and bound in Great Britain by The Cromwell Press Ltd, Trowbridge, Wilts.

Contents

Authors and Contributors   vi

Acknowledgements   vii

Introduction   1

1   What is citizenship education?   4

2   Citizenship and the whole curriculum   20

3   Implementing citizenship education:
    A curriculum case study   38

4   Curriculum projects in citizenship   56

5   Teaching and learning in citizenship   70

6   Experiential learning in the community   85

7   Resources and citizenship education   101

8   Assessing citizenship education   123

Conclusion   145

References and further reading   147

Index   151

Authors

James Arthur is Professor of Education and Head of Educational Research at Canterbury Christ Church University College. He has written extensively on teaching and learning in the secondary school and is currently a member of the DfEE's Citizenship Teacher Training and CPD Group.

Daniel Wright is a graduate of St John's College, Cambridge and teaches at Gordon's School in Surrey.

Contributors

Ian Potter is a deputy headteacher of Ousedale School, which is a Beacon Comprehensive and he served on the Teacher Training Citizenship Committee of the Teacher Training Agency.

David Leddington is a senior lecturer in education at Canterbury Christ Church University College. He has developed a number of resources for secondary school teaching.

Ruth Tudor is a former principal subject officer of the QCA and head of history in a Hackney school. She has written and developed resources for teaching in secondary schools.

Acknowledgements

We would like to thank the following for permission to print materials written by them or their organisations: John Potter (CSV), Don Rowe (Citizenship Foundation), Professor Audrey Osler (Centre for Citizenship Studies in Education at Leicester University), Gabby Rowberry (Council for Education in World Citizenship) and Randy Metcalf (Institute for Citizenship) together with John Lloyd of Birmingham Education Authority and Lachlan MacCallum HMI at the Scottish Office in Edinburgh.

Introduction

Citizenship, both the subject and the practice, should be a bridge between the vocational aims of education and education for its own sake... Not all of life is productive:
there is leisure, there is culture, both of which active citizens can defend, indeed
enhance.

(Bernard Crick 2000)

Every secondary school in England is required to prepare a plan for the implementation
of the Citizenship Order for August 2002. At Key Stages 1 and 2, non-statutory guidance
indicates that citizenship education should be integrated with personal, social and health
education. The plan in secondary schools should build on what is already being done in
citizenship education and its preparation should be flexible enough to allow schools to
decide how to plan for it, what teaching and learning approaches to use and what assessment techniques are most appropriate – all so long as the programmes of study in citizenship education are met. Citizenship education will remain a contested subject and
schools will adopt different curriculum approaches for different purposes, they will also
have different ideas and notions about what citizenship education is about. This is to be
expected and the intention of the Citizenship Order is to set out a framework, as Crick
says:

Being a statutory order, that is to say a legally enforceable document, it contains only a
formal statement of aims and only an implied justification; it carries no advice about
the methods of delivery, learning techniques nor teaching methods appropriate to citizenship.... The virtue of the order is that the generality of its prescriptions will leave
the school and the teacher with a good deal of freedom and discretion, more than in
other statutory subjects.

(Crick 2000: 117)

We could interpret this to mean that citizenship education is a 'light touch' subject order.

However, the rhetoric of government clearly intends to develop the notion of 'education with character' in every secondary school and seeks to use citizenship education to reinforce this character education. The Green Paper *Schools: Building on Success* (DfEE 2001) defines this 'education with character' as consisting of pupils learning 'to know right from wrong; to get along with their fellow pupils, whatever their background; to work in a team; to make a contribution to the school as a community; and to develop positive attitudes to life and work' (DfEE 2001: 61). Citizenship education is specifically mentioned as contributing to this educational aim by helping to develop 'habits of mind' in pupils. This 'New Labour' thinking appears to follow Wil Kymlicka's (1999: 79–97) ideas on citizenship education in which it is about the inculcation of particular habits, virtues and identities. For Kymlicka:

> Citizenship education is not just a matter of learning the basic facts about the institutions and procedures of political life; it also involves acquiring a range of dispositions, virtues and loyalties that are intimately bound up with the practice of democratic citizenship.
>
> (Kymlicka 1999)

This view differs little from the government's and is far from a 'light touch' and more a set of principles or goals that shape the entire school curriculum. Of course the problem is trying to articulate what these 'citizenship' virtues look like and how they can be taught, even if only a functional consensus can be agreed upon in the context of a school education.

The aim of this book is to help student teachers and those teachers who are new to citizenship education to develop an understanding of teaching and learning about citizenship education with a clear emphasis on classroom practice. We aim to engage in discussion and debate about the ways in which the different approaches to citizenship impact on initial teacher education and also how this will form part of a process of development and dissemination of good practices in the application of citizenship to the continuing professional development of teachers. It is not intended to provide the definitive answer to the delivery of citizenship in schools as there will naturally be a number of diverse approaches to the subject. Teachers will recognise that they can and must use their own professional independence to ensure flexibility in approach and that they alone must decide what to do in response to the challenges of this new subject in the school curriculum. We are aware that you will be teaching in different situations and contexts and therefore we have tried to make this book as relevant as possible to your needs. We are also aware that it is most unlikely that you will be a member of a citizenship education department – it is more likely that you will be the sole teacher in your school teaching the subject. This means that you will need to rely a great deal on your own ideas and talents. Your subject knowledge may not cover the full range of the Citizenship Order and you may therefore need to address these gaps by acquiring further political, moral and social understanding together with professional knowledge about schools and involvement with communities. This book has not been written to resolve these gaps in knowledge, but rather as a pragmatic introduction to teaching citizenship education itself. By combining some theoretical and policy discussions we highlight the differing views on citizenship education and suggest texts for further reading. At the end of each chapter a set of tasks or points to discuss and reflect on is provided. We also offer suggestions for practical teaching and assessment. However, it is vitally important that you learn to experiment with these suggestions and develop your own ideas for planning for learning in citizenship education. The suggestions we make are for you to consider and adapt and to vary any of the recommended ideas, materials or resources to meet your own particular needs.

Chapter one describes what citizenship education means in the context of the Citizenship Order while chapter two discusses different approaches to citizenship education in the curriculum. In chapter three Ian Potter, a deputy headteacher, provides a personal view by offering a case study of the implementation of citizenship education into his own school. Chapter four describes and discusses a number of curriculum projects in citizenship education organised by the Coalition for Citizenship Education, the QCA and the DfEE. Chapter five provides an introduction to the teaching methods which may be employed to teach citizenship education and examines some pedagogical issues peculiar to citizenship education. Chapter six introduces community experiential learning and explores ways of involving pupils in community participation. In chapter seven David Leddington reviews the use of resources in citizenship teaching and in chapter eight Ruth Tudor looks at how best to assess citizenship education in the classroom. Both David and Ruth are currently editing a text entitled *Resources for the Teaching of Citizenship in the Secondary School*, which has been especially prepared to complement this present text. James Arthur and Daniel Wright have had overall editorial control of this book, but the contributing authors are essentially responsible for the content of their chapters.

CHAPTER 1

What is citizenship education?

The increasingly complex nature of our society, the greater cultural diversity and the apparent loss of a value consensus, combined with the collapse of traditional support mechanisms such as extended families, mean that there has never been a greater need for schools to address the task of introducing young people to the rights and responsibilities of citizenship and the values on which concepts of law and justice rest.

(Citizenship Foundation 1994: 59)

Introduction

Teachers are invariably concerned with more than the acquisition of knowledge and skills for they also have a commitment, whether explicit or not, to the acquisition of desirable values. Values here refer in their most general sense to that which is good and worthwhile, particularly desirable qualities of character such as honesty, integrity, altruism, justice, respect and so on. While teachers are likely to agree that their aim is to free pupils to think for themselves, they are less sure of the formative role they exercise on the civic, moral and social development of their pupils. Teachers know that in order to educate their pupils they must first have an idea of what they are aiming to do, of what education is. Teaching is not a neutral activity and teachers still help shape some of the values and virtues that their pupils learn in school. Values are essentially about dispositions and consist of cognitive and affective dimensions and consequently often lack a behavioural element. Citizenship education is about action and may be said to be about the activation of values and dispositions. It does include a much more explicit behavioural dimension since active citizenship is observable in one's conduct. This requires an altogether larger perspective than current teacher training courses afford their students, for what is really required is a philosophy of human nature – an idea of what human beings are and what they might become. The social aspects of human nature are not static, but developmental and will vary between time and place in response to different contexts. However, what pupils 'might become' is obviously still both a controversial and contested subject for teachers and members of society in general.

In the same way, notions of citizenship are rightly contested for they depend on different ideas about how society should be governed and organised. This again presupposes what human nature is and what human beings ought to become – 'good' citizens? This in turn will depend on our assumptions, beliefs, experiences, convictions and limitations. Recent research on what teachers perceive to be 'good citizenship' found that they overwhelmingly felt that a 'good citizen' is one who exhibits social concern and tolerance for others and has a marked disposition towards moral behaviour and community involvement (Davies, Gregory and Riley 1999: 57). Notions of citizenship are also historically and culturally conditioned and context specific. Definitions and propositions in respective theories of citizenship therefore vary over time and between societies. Citizenship is an extremely complex concept and consists of a range of legal, moral, social, political and cultural elements. In educating someone for membership of a society we are effectively nurturing a sense of what that person should become. In England the historical manifestations of citizenship have resulted from the intersection of a particular political perspective with a particular educational outlook. Today the central political issue in education is how we educate pupils for a pluralist society in the traditions of civil society while simultaneously preparing them to participate in the shaping of that society. Citizenship education has become a major device for implementing this aim, but it needs to be recognised at the outset that it is a complex enterprise with new challenges and questions being posed for the teacher.

Objectives

At the end of this chapter you should:

1. know and understand why there is a need for pupils to learn about citizenship;
2. know and understand what the new directions and dimensions of citizenship education are;
3. be clear about the meaning and application of citizenship education; and
4. be aware of the new requirements for citizenship education in the National Curriculum

Theoretical background

Citizenship education in the late 1990s reached the top of the political agenda as a result of a number of civic and social concerns. A range of research data appeared to confirm what many had already assumed or suspected: that there were deteriorating social and cultural conditions in England and that political and voluntary participation in the affairs of society was in decline. It was found that community networks were breaking down and that there was less trust of and responsibility to our neighbours and even less trust in the institutions of society itself. This breakdown in social norms was especially marked among the young and manifested itself in anti-social behaviour, increased truancy and exclusions from schools, high teenage pregnancy levels and increased alienation from the political processes of democratic society. Moral and civic values appeared to be lacking in school pupils and there was much discussion of a 'social recession' or 'deficit in civil society'. Citizenship education was recognised once again as a possible solution to these social ills; once again, because it was not the first time that it had been considered necessary as a result of a perceived decline in moral direction in the young and a perceived weakening in the social institutions of society.

Frederick Swann's *Primer of English Citizenship*, published in 1918, as 'a plain guide to right action' (p. vii) was a response to the aftermath of the First World War. The book was concerned with building the moral character of the young and was very much a sort of new religion, a rational secular morality. There is a strong link between the advocacy of citizenship education and a perceived decline or crisis in the moral standards of society. This was why the first pressure group for citizenship education, called the Association for Education in Citizenship, was formed in 1934. In reality though it can be argued that citizenship education is not and never has been a new curriculum initiative – it has been around for as long as the state has had formal responsibility for the provision of schools. Consequently, every school in England up until the late 1950s was responding in some way to the educational goal of developing 'good' citizens. The importance of citizenship as a legal status was clearly reinforced in the British Nationality Act 1981 which linked this status with membership of the political entity of the UK. However, Gilbert (1996: 60) warns us not to focus on the legal status of the citizen but instead stresses democratic participation which is a view of citizenship education which engages the interest and commitment of young people and motivates them to participate in decision making. Citizenship therefore becomes a practice rather than a status. Which is why Kerr (1999: 25–6) reminds us that the definition of citizenship education together with the location of it, the approaches we adopt, who is involved, how it is resourced and what outcomes we expect are all questions that need to be discussed.

In the 1990s there were also concerns about how young people saw themselves as members of society and as part of the nation. In one research project comparing French and English children's notions of citizenship it was discovered that French children freely spoke of their emotional attachment to their country and that what made them proud to be French was French civilisation and history (Broadfoot *et al.* 2000). In contrast, English children were much more diffident in attitude and spoke about the sporting prowess of the English, their ability to speak English and not being poor as evidence of their superiority over others. Clearly, French children had a high level of pride in their national identity and culture and the idea of them being citizens was very much an everyday matter. French schools have always had a statutory duty placed on them by the State to produce citizens who understand and respect the constitution and the values of freedom, equality and solidarity. Policy makers in England had a mass of data at their hands to suggest that English society was somehow under threat and that political awareness was very low. Citizenship education was again considered to be a possible answer and policy makers saw in it a way to re-emphasise responsibility and duty, community membership and the promotion of the common good among the young.

However, there was no consensus on what citizenship education meant and it was recognised that without a broad-based working definition it would be impossible to introduce it into schools. There was also a feeling among some that citizenship education already occurred in schools through the indirect transmission of values which the school ethos provided and therefore much was in any case being done to build the moral and social character of pupils. Attempts to define and promote citizenship education have a long history in England and stretch from the *Anglorum Praelia*, a school textbook ordered to be used in the reign of Elizabeth I which extolled the military prowess of the English, to the New Labour notion of good citizenship in the 21st century which is seen as widening the scope of service to our neighbours and meeting the needs of the emerging new economy. In recent times a range of organisations have promoted a national discussion of policy on citizenship and these include: The Citizenship Foundation, The Citizenship Institute, Community Volunteers Service, Council for Education in World Citizenship and the Hansard Society. These bodies have formed the Coalition of Citizenship Organisations and have had considerable impact on policy makers in the promotion and implementation of citizenship education in schools.

In 1990 the Speaker of the House of Commons chaired a Commission on Citizenship which published a report, *Encouraging Citizenship*. This made certain recommendations on ways of facilitating *social* citizenship through schools, voluntary efforts and public services. In the same year the National Curriculum Council published guidance for schools on how to develop education for citizenship and advocated 'participative citizenship'. Both documents attempted to define citizenship, the first calling it 'social citizenship' while the second referred to it as 'education for citizenship'. There was still no consensus about the purposes or approaches to citizenship education. For example, Derek Heater (1990) characterises citizenship by five key perspectives which he lists as: identity, civil citizenship, political citizenship, social citizenship and civic virtue, and he concludes that citizenship is only one among many identities of an individual.

In addition, Don Rowe (2000: 194–203) of the Foundation for Citizenship outlined at least eight varying standpoints in citizenship education which he claims are competing with each other. They are the constitutional knowledge, the patriotic, the parental, the religious, the values conflict or pluralist, the emphatic, the school ethos and the community action approaches. Rowe argues that while some of these notions of citizenship overlap with each other, some are incompatible with pluralism. Other approaches could be mentioned, such as the post-modern or feminist citizen, but together they indicate the wide range of thinking on what citizenship education is and can be. There is also the possibility of exclusion from the benefits of citizenship as a result of poverty, class, gender or race which is also well covered in the literature (see Morris 1994). It can be seen that no single version of citizenship enjoys predominance in the debate and that there are indeed many diverse and different formulations of citizenship current, but these different emphases are not always necessarily incompatible with each other.

Penny Enslin understands citizenship to comprise five related features:

> First, citizenship bestows on an individual the status of membership of a territorially defined political unit in which reciprocal rights and responsibilities are exercised on equal terms with fellow citizens. Second, citizenship confers identity on an individual, an awareness of self as a member of a collective.... This identity includes, third, a set of values, usually interpreted as comprising a commitment to the common good.... Citizenship in a democracy involves, fourth, a degree of participation in the life of the polity... fifth, knowledge and understanding of political and legal principles....
>
> (Enslin 2000: 149)

Enslin believes that all five features of citizenship have important implications for education, particularly in the promotion of democracy. The specific promotion of identity and values were identified as problematic and less clear in their connection with education. Nevertheless, usage of citizenship concepts in schools is often muddled with no unanimity in the area that has led some to believe that any precise definition is almost impossible. Citizenship education is therefore an emerging concept, but we can clarify a number of clear strands within it. First, citizenship education is concerned with three levels: the local community, national citizenship and international citizenship. All three levels are essential components of citizenship education. Second, citizenship education is a combination of approaches which could be summarised as:

1. **education *about* citizenship** – knowledge of the political system operating in England, the UK and Europe;
2. **education *for* citizenship** – the development of skills and values as a means to encourage active citizens;
3. **education *through* citizenship** – emphasis on learning by doing through experiences in and out of school.

There is obviously a great deal of overlap between these three expressions of citizenship in schools, but citizenship education is the term used by the government's Advisory Group on Education for Citizenship and the Teaching of Democracy which produced a final report in 1998. This advisory group was chaired by Professor Bernard Crick – a staunch supporter of citizenship education in schools, and it produced a broad definition of citizenship together with a framework and approach for schools. The working definition used was based on T. H. Marshall's classic definition which has become the starting point for all subsequent discussions on the topic. He distinguishes three phases of citizenship – namely the civil, the political and the social. Marshall first emphasised the civil rights necessary for freedom and identified the law courts as the characteristic institutions for safeguarding them. Second, he emphasised the rights to participate in the exercise of political power and the characteristic institution identified is the elected assembly. Finally, he emphasised social rights as concerned with the welfare state, with the characteristic institutions being the social services, health and education. Marshall was writing at the time the welfare state was being built and therefore he believed that the extension of political rights led to the extension of social rights through redistribution. Consequently, many of the assumptions of Marshall, such as full employment and the stable nuclear family, are no longer modern realities for most. All the members of Crick's advisory group agreed that citizenship education consisted of the same three inter-related areas, but they refined their definition along the following lines.

Social and moral responsibility

Here, the advisory group held that, central to any definition of effective, or, more precisely, good citizenship is an individual's sense of social and moral responsibility. As a result, pupils must be encouraged to develop their understanding of the moral values which should shape and guide their actions within a pluralist and democratic society. This social and moral responsibility finds its reflection in behaviour that is just and fair. Examples of this could include the mutual respect and consideration that pupils have for both themselves and those around them, whether within the classroom, school or wider community. Further, it is expressed in behaviour appropriate to the context in which pupils find themselves. Respect for authority within both the school and wider community is an important aspect of this. Pupils would also learn through this aspect of citizenship a sense of what is right and wrong and an informed understanding of the choices available to them and the consequences of such choices. In practice, the advisory group explains that it should result in pupils who are aware of the choices open to them, able to come to informed decisions and to accept responsibility for such choices.

Community involvement

The advisory group defined 'community involvement' as positive involvement in and service to the life and concerns of both the school community and the communities beyond it. These, it suggests, can be at local, national or global levels. For the group, positive involvement is not necessarily political; it can be reflected in participation in non-partisan groups, such as voluntary bodies, working with public authorities, publicising, fundraising or in negotiating with others to achieve a desired and desirable end. This end, it makes explicit, must in some way benefit or improve the community with which it is concerned.

Political literacy

Here, the advisory group define political literacy, in part, as an understanding of the institutions of representative government and the various methods through which opinion can most effectively and healthily be expressed. But the term 'political literacy' is for them not restricted merely to an understanding of political knowledge; it is intended to include knowledge of and preparation for 'public life' in a more general sense. Preparation for public life involves knowledge of effective negotiation and compromise, and responsible decision making based upon the realities of contemporary economic and social problems. Employment, taxation and the allocation of public resources all fall within the group's definition of political literacy. Such political, economic and social issues should, it suggests, be discussed from local, national and global perspectives.

In summary, the Crick Report identified a series of concepts and values which it believed underpinned citizenship education, including:

- quality and diversity;
- law and human rights;
- the common good;
- rights and responsibilities;
- power and authority;
- freedom and order;
- conflict and cooperation;
- individuals and society;
- democracy; and
- the rule of law and justice.

The government response to the advisory group's recommendations was both positive and multifaceted. First, in the revised 1999 National Curriculum New Labour gave a renewed emphasis to the civic, moral and social aims of the school curriculum in its Statement of Values, Aims and Purposes which accompanied the new Subject Orders. The 1988 Education Reform Act had simply stated that the aims of the curriculum in all publicly funded schools was the 'spiritual, moral, cultural, mental and physical development' of pupils. The curriculum was seen as basically intellectual and moral in character and an academic curriculum was formulated which included most of the traditional subjects as a hierarchy of disciplines. The new statutory statement goes much further and includes the development of children's social responsibility, their community involvement, the development of effective relationships, the knowledge and understanding of society, their participation in the affairs of society, their respect for others and their contribution to the building up of the common good, including their development of independence and self-esteem. Second, a new area of the curriculum was to be a statutory requirement from September 2002 in all secondary schools – namely citizenship education – and a Citizenship Order was incorporated into the National Curriculum.

The Citizenship Order

The Citizenship Order itself details the requirements that are to be met in all publicly funded schools throughout England. It sets out the programmes of study, the attainment targets and end of key stage descriptions in addition to reserving judgement on the way in which attainment will be assessed until such time as it has been decided exactly how assessment will be carried out. At Key Stages 3 and 4, the programme of study breaks down into three distinct areas:

- knowledge and understanding about becoming informed citizens;
- developing skills of enquiry and communication;
- developing skills of participation and responsible action.

The order emphasises that 'teaching should ensure that knowledge and understanding about becoming informed citizens are acquired and applied when developing skills of enquiry and communication, and participation and responsible action'. In short, it maintains that the knowledge about citizenship is best acquired through the skills of citizenship.

Although ostensibly there is much overlap between the content of the programmes of study at Key Stages 3 and 4, the main difference is found in approach. Broadly speaking, the programme of study at Key Stage 3 is descriptive, whereas that at Key Stage 4 is analytical. This stems from the obvious need to enable the pupils to acquire the raw knowledge at Key Stage 3 before they can reasonably be expected to analyse it at Key Stage 4. The programmes of study boil down to an understanding of the legal rights and responsibilities of individuals and of the apparatus which defines, enforces and protects such legal rights, as well as the way in which such rights have been and can continue to be abused. These include an understanding of what representative government means and the machinery through which representation can be enacted. The role of the media in this process is considered at both key stages as is an appreciation of the role of the United Kingdom within a European and global context. The only main points of departure in content between the two key stages concerns a study of labour relations and finance and the economy at Key Stage 4.

The order also sets out the way in which education about citizenship is attained as a result of education through citizenship. Those aspects of the programme of study that achieve this are: developing the skills of enquiry and communication, and developing the skills of participation and responsible action. This ensures that teaching and learning methods focus on the active as opposed to what had previously been more passive methods of simply acquiring knowledge. At both Key Stages 3 and 4 the education through citizenship approach is largely similar, with more intensive intellectual involvement being expected at Key Stage 3 than at Key Stage 4. In the enquiry and communication aspect, for example, pupils are called upon to 'think', 'justify' and 'contribute' at Key Stage 3, whereas at Key Stage 4 they are expected to 'research' and 'express, justify and defend'. In the skills of participation and responsible action section of the programme of study, the key words of 'imagine', 'negotiate' and 'reflect' are exactly the same. We would recommend that you read McLaughlin (2000) and Garratt (2000) who provide excellent philosophical critiques of the Citizenship Education Order.

In considering the aims of both the National Curriculum and the Citizenship Order it can be seen that citizenship education focuses both on political and social literacy. The government is effectively urging a 'civic morality' and placing emphasis on putting aside personal interests for the sake of the community. New Labour seeks to balance the social good of the community against the good of the individual and at the same time emphasises the role of 'mediating institutions', such as churches and trade unions, in addition to schools, in the belief that society as a whole is educative. The aim is to strengthen the democratic and participative spirit within each individual and therefore motivate them to contribute positively to the wider society. Much of New Labour's rhetoric is based on a communitarian approach to education which emphasises inclusive language like 'One Nation'. Nevertheless, there is also an emphasis on pluralism – the recognition of the worth of difference and the right to maintain a multiple identity while enjoying the rights of a full citizen.

The social and moral dimensions of citizenship education have to be experienced as meaningful if they are to be lived. Indeed, the social and moral dimensions are preconditions for both the civic and political dimensions of citizenship. Concern with the social and moral education of pupils is not a recent interest, but changes within society have accelerated the social demands made upon schools. At the very least, society expects teachers and schools to correct the behaviour of their pupils and to teach them moral and social values which usually means insisting on 'good' behaviour. The social and moral development of pupils has thus assumed a much greater place in the aspiration of schools. Programmes of personal, social and moral education, together with attempts at citizenship education, invariably emphasise a range of social skills and these skills are introduced early and built upon throughout the years of schooling. A pupil's sense and ability to make socially and morally productive decisions do not develop by themselves; rather, they require knowledge, values and skills. Above all, opportunities are required for pupils to experience social relations and indeed become the kinds of human beings we expect within the social context of community. Teachers themselves are very much role models of what it is to be a good human being and a citizen. However, pupils also need to be able to operate critically and become informed and ethically empowered active citizens.

Social and moral education are clearly both a prerequisite for and essential requirements of citizenship education. They involve learning a series of social and moral skills and developing a knowledge base from which to understand and interpret the range of social and moral issues which citizens must address in their lives. It involves the ability to interact with others in ways that are socially and ethically acceptable or valued. Children are not born reliable, trustworthy, responsible and considerate – these qualities are shaped by daily habits of thought and action through their social experiences. Education is unavoidably a social and moral engagement and schools are a rich source of social and moral values for the pupil. As Carr and Steutel conclude:

> positive moral and other human development is as much, if not more, a matter of right affective nurture and good example and support from parents and community, than of the disinterested mastery of rational principles of duty and obligation... virtuous conduct requires the kind of sensitive independent judgement which cannot be secured by mechanical adherence to general rules or precepts.
>
> (Carr and Steutel 1999: 252)

This reminds us that social and moral dimensions of citizenship education are not simply about knowledge or learning rules, but must be experienced and indeed lived.

The aim of community involvement as a dimension of citizenship education is linked with pupils learning the meaning of social interdependence and democratic principles. Every pupil's education should include experiential learning of the kind offered by community service. Again many consider it to be an indispensable prerequisite of citizenship education and cite many benefits for it. Few English schools organise any sustained or integrated community service experiences for their pupils. Citizenship education is intimately linked with the essential nature of morality, community and identity and will therefore be a contested life-skills subject area. Citizenship is bound up with participation in community but there are a number of key issues to be resolved. The following are included among them:

1. What are the teaching and learning elements of community involvement?
2. How do we measure the success of effective pupil participation within and beyond the school?
3. How do we build successful networks and partnerships with local communities for community involvement?
4. How can we use community involvement to promote a sense of citizenship and to build stronger communities?

5. How do we train teachers to:
   a. coordinate community involvement;
   b. plan and evaluate community involvement;
   c. assess learning from community involvement;
   d. manage pupils' active learning through community involvement;
   e. liase with voluntary agencies in community involvement?

Some may accuse New Labour of 'party politics', but the political order in English society is much broader than party politics and involves a greater spectrum of activities. In a very narrow sense politics is simply about gaining and exercising power in government at whatever level. In a broader sense it is about influencing the exercise of power, public policy and the structures of civil society through protest and membership of organised pressure groups. In an even broader sense it is about adopting a general philosophy of life – a moral vision for society, perhaps. It can therefore range from participation in public debate to service in elected office. Few can object to an education in schools which encourages all of these. Political literacy is certainly broader than political knowledge, as Crick and Porter say:

> A politically literate person will know what the main political disputes are about; what beliefs the main contestants have of them; how they are likely to affect him; and he will have a predisposition to try to do something about it in a manner at once effective and respectful of the sincerity of others.
>
> (Crick and Porter 1990: 33)

Crick later refined this to: 'the ultimate test of political literacy lies in creating a proclivity to action not in achieving more theoretical analysis' (Crick and Lister 1978: 41). Pupils need to learn how to engage and participate in public life, not just learn about it.

The National Curriculum Order for Citizenship does not mention political literacy and some may consequently allow a slippage from political literacy in favour of personal and social elements as the main carrier of citizenship education. However, a careful reading of the whole National Curriculum indicates that there is a clear expectation that political literacy should be taught and in some way experienced as meaningful.

Citizenship education in Scotland

As Scotland is an integral part of Great Britain it is interesting to consider how citizenship education is treated in comparison with England. The first observation that might be made is that there appears to be no haste to introduce a discrete subject called 'citizenship education' into Scottish schools. Indeed, in contrast to England there is a real desire in

Scotland to seek as much discussion and consultation with parents, teachers and pupils before any response to citizenship education is made. There is also the important observation that in Scottish schools modern studies is taught to pupils in their first two years and becomes an option thereafter. The content of modern studies consists largely of the political literacy elements identified in the Crick Report, but also includes social and moral questions and issues which make a major contribution to the development of knowledge and skills related to citizenship. This perhaps explains why there is no immediate need to address citizenship education in Scottish schools. However, the Scottish Executive have produced, through its agency, Learning and Teaching in Scotland, a paper for consultation called *Education for Citizenship in Scotland* (Scottish Executive). This paper is a national statement on education for citizenship, but it is not a definitive statement, nor does it suggest any particular coverage for the school curriculum. The paper advances a broad view of citizenship education along the following lines:

> Each person, regardless of age or socio-economic position, belongs to various types of community, both communities of place, from local to global, and communities of interest, rooted in a common concern or purpose. Citizenship involves enjoying rights and exercising responsibilities in these various types of community. This way of seeing citizenship encompasses the specific idea of political participation by members of a democratic state. It also includes the more general notion that citizenship embraces a range of participatory activities, not all overtly political, that affect the welfare of communities.
>
> (Scottish Executive 2000: 2)

The paper includes references to the positive contribution of voluntary bodies in society and also raises the notion of cultural citizenship which appears to be given less attention in England. Another difference is the greater emphasis in the Scottish paper on critical thinking. The paper makes clear that responsible citizenship should be characterised by:

a) an ability and disposition to examine matters critically and to develop informed views, including views that challenge established conventions and the status quo;
b) the ability and willingness to think creatively and act appropriately in response to a situation;
c) sensitivity to other people's needs and views and consideration of the potential impacts of choices and actions on others and on the environment;
d) the ability and willingness to exercise rights and to act for the benefit of others;
e) the ability and willingness to work with others to achieve a common purpose imbued with a shared sense of social and environmental responsibility; and
f) a disposition to openness, objectivity and rejection of prejudice or discrimination.

The authors of the paper, which was chaired by Professor Pamela Munn of Edinburgh University, came to the view that:

> the response to this situation should not be to stipulate any single course of study of 'citizenship education' as part of each student's core programme. Such an approach has a number of drawbacks. In practical terms, it would have the effect of restricting the scope for student choice and flexibility of provision and could also create practical difficulties for curriculum planning in the post-14 stages. Most importantly, to appear to locate 'citizenship education' in one particular post-14 course of study would be inconsistent with the broad view of education for citizenship being advanced in this paper.
>
> (Scottish Executive 2000)

This review group viewed citizenship education as integral to the education of students and consisting in the whole curriculum and ethos of the school. The intention was to establish a broadly based capability of active citizenship in each individual and that this capability would be rooted in knowledge and understanding together with a range of generic skills and competences including personal qualities and dispositions. There is emphasis on young people as citizens, not becoming citizens, and therefore there is little notion of preparing children for citizenship. Interestingly, the debate about the citizenship consultation was conducted on the internet where the quality of debate is displayed for all to see. Further developments are awaited. In Wales, citizenship education is not yet a separate policy proposal and is viewed as forming part of the general personal and social education programmes in Welsh schools.

Conclusion

The government has established a Citizenship Education Working Party, which is charged with providing guidelines for schools on the types of questions raised above. Schools will be issued with these guidelines in 2001, but it still remains the case that each school will plan and execute its own citizenship education programmes in the way it chooses. However, as schools organise their own provision of citizenship education they will require commitment and participation from their pupils which is no easy task to achieve. Pupils will need to be motivated, which will require new and imaginative approaches to teaching and learning. In addition, pupils should be involved in deciding on, planning and carrying out community involvement activities as well as experiencing some aspects of democratic practices within their own school environment. Citizenship education may offer schools innovative and imaginative ways for school improvement; social inclusion and learning through experience in community should provide greater opportunities for reflection so that effective citizens can demonstrate positive outcomes.

Tasks

TASK 1.1 (A)

An extremely good introduction to notions of national identity is provided by Professor Linda Colley's book, Britons: Forging the Nation 1707–1837. What kind of national identity is described and advocated in her book? Is she right to claim that British identity depended on the Protestantism, imperialism and continental conflicts of the 18th and 19th centuries and with their passing, British identity has weakened and unravelled? Is British identity merely an 'invented tradition'? Britain has no written constitution. Britain is also a monarchy and many would argue that citizenship is essentially a republican concept. What changes are necessary, if any, for the reform of the monarchy and constitution to make the concept of citizenship easier to understand in the modern age? Is the old idea of the relationship between sovereign and subject outdated?

TASK 1.1 (B)

The Runneymede Trust published a controversial report in 2000 entitled Commission on the Future of Multi-Ethnic Britain. The report concluded that many images of Britishness are often southern-English centred and that Britishness itself may be racially coded. While commenting that Britishness is not ideal, the report concludes that it [Britishness] 'appears acceptable, particularly when suitably qualified'. The report boldly asks: does Britishness as such have a future? There are questions for citizenship education in this report including: do children in your classes have multiple-identities? Are they conscious of these identities? How are they expressed? Would it be better to speak of modern Britain in terms of a 'community of communities'? Should citizenship teachers actively attempt to promote an 'understanding of equality difference'? What would this look like in both teaching and content?

TASK 1.1 (C)

In South Africa a recent report (2000) entitled Values, Education and Democracy by the government's Working Group on Values in Education recommended that each pupil in school should declare a weekly pledge or vow at assembly to serve as a reminder of the fundamental values to which South Africans in a democracy aspire. The proposed pledge they suggested was:

'I promise to be loyal to my country, South Africa, and to do my best to promote its welfare and the well-being of all of its citizens. I promise to respect all of my fellow citizens and all of our various traditions. Let us work for peace, friendship and reconciliation and heal the scars left by past conflicts, and let us build a common destiny together.'

The schooling provided for all citizens in a democracy is not neutral – it promotes personal values – and some would argue that it also promotes a 'national character'. Could we have such a pledge in Britain ritually repeated at weekly school assemblies? Or, is this simply the promotion of the 'cult of the State' and, what would the implications of this be?

TASK 1.2

Below is a quotation from Professor Bernard Crick, Chairman of the Citizenship Advisory Group, the organisation responsible for defining and recommending exactly what nature education for citizenship should take in schools. Here, he defines the aims of citizenship education. Consider the validity of these aims and how far they are capable of addressing his concerns about the 'current health' of democracy in England.

We aim at no less than a change in the political culture of this country both nationally and locally; for people to think of themselves as active citizens, willing, able and equipped to have an influence in public life and with critical capacities to weigh evidence before speaking and acting; to build on and to extend radically to young people the best in existing traditions of community involvement and public service, and to make them individually confident in finding new forms of involvement and action among themselves. There are worrying levels of apathy, ignorance and cynicism about public life. These, unless tackled at every level, could well diminish the hoped for benefits both of constitutional reform and of the changing nature of the welfare state.

TASK 1.3

The content of citizenship education programmes can be taught and learnt in many ways. Conduct an audit of your school's current citizenship education provision and then list the key attitudes, concepts, knowledge and skills of citizenship education which are already taught and learnt in your school. Now list the key attitudes, concepts, knowledge and skills which are still required to meet the demands of the Citizenship Order. How would you seek to bridge the gap? Remember that teaching citizenship education is not simply about content.

CHAPTER 2

Citizenship and the whole curriculum

What is not ruled in is not ruled out; therefore so long as everything in the order [citizenship] is covered to a basic level of understanding, such topics can be stressed more than others and used as gateways into the whole curriculum.

(Crick 2000: 118)

Introduction

The curriculum represents all the planned experiences which a school offers its pupils, but ultimately it is concerned with helping to develop human beings as members of society. In a very real sense the curriculum is about 'who we ought to become' and this cannot be done in isolation, but requires participation in a community. Each school's curriculum provides pupils with a range of opportunities to participate in society and to maximise their potential as human beings within a social context. School curricula are based on relationships which provide opportunities for cooperation, participation and shared responsibility within a community, which is, of itself, educative. It is concerned with the relationship between the school and the wider community and the preparation of the pupil for life beyond school. This encouragement of active participation in community is fundamental to the pupils' growth and development as unique human beings since both human nature and education demand interaction between communities. A school community is intrinsic to all the experiences across the taught curriculum and it helps facilitate sharing. The school's values, aims and ethos are also indicative of a sense of shared purpose. It is the curriculum which communicates, through explicit and implicit messages, the common culture or notion of citizenship which many schools seek to achieve. Consequently, the school curriculum requires a vision of education in order that the desired objectives – academic, moral, social, civic and personal experiences – are fostered for the growth of each pupil.

Since citizenship education is now a statutory subject of the National Curriculum, schools will need to reinforce and incorporate it both into the life of the school and into the everyday practices of the individual teachers. There are a number of different curriculum approaches to citizenship education and it is for each school to determine which is most appropriate for them. As the DfEE says: 'It is for schools to choose how they organise their school curriculum to include the programmes of study for citizenship' (DfEE/QCA 1999: 6). Both the formal curriculum and the ethos of the school will therefore need to contribute to citizenship education in a clearly articulated way. Some believe that citizenship education has the potential to be a vehicle for school development by reflecting on the existing curriculum and looking anew at teacher development. However, individual schools will make their own decisions about how it is implemented, at least initially, and they will need to consider adopting a coherent approach. This chapter does not address the teaching or assessment of citizenship education in the planning process as this is dealt with in later chapters.

Objectives

By the end of this chapter you will have understood:

- that the school's core values, community and ethos are essential elements in citizenship education;
- that all subjects within the school curriculum make a contribution to citizenship education;
- that citizenship education can be a distinct subject on its own;
- that a whole-school approach to effective citizenship education is necessary; and
- ways of planning for citizenship and reflecting on your own school's values in relation to the implementation of citizenship education.

Curriculum approaches

Governors, headteachers and senior management within each school need to reflect on the implications of planning for citizenship education. One important conclusion that they should reach early on is that no single approach can be relied upon to deliver citizenship education and that there are clear benefits and disadvantages to the range of approaches on offer. Since the implementation of citizenship is adaptable to a variety of school cultures, the management team need to consider which approach is appropriate to the unique flavour of their own school.

They also need to recognise that it is almost impossible for any one subject to cover all that is required in teaching citizenship education. Different perspectives in citizenship are needed from all the subject areas together with their different subject content and modes of teaching. A whole-school approach is effectively needed which will require in turn a management strategy which involves all the staff and direct consultation with pupils in designing an appropriate strategy. Research has already indicated that teachers are generally eager to participate in citizenship education since they are committed to making the world a 'better' place for their pupils and they also wish to assist in the process of their pupils becoming 'good citizens' (Davies 1999: 81). Other research (Trafford 1997) indicates that when pupils are really involved in their school, academic standards are raised and pupils feel valued. As a result they are more likely to participate in their own learning.

It will be for the whole-school community to decide what practices need to be changed in order to achieve the desired goals of citizenship education. Some schools emphasise the general quality of their strong community, the friendly and caring relationships among staff and pupils, their recognition of individual needs and their safe and supportive learning environment as evidence that they are already involved in citizenship education. Of course this will depend largely upon the health of the school as an institution and on the morale of staff. Other schools will point to the contribution of various subjects in the curriculum, including personal and social education (PSE), as evidence of their contribution to citizenship education, while perhaps a minority of schools will focus exclusively on the provision of citizenship education as a separate subject in the school curriculum. Whatever approach is adopted the governors and teachers of a school will need to consider whether the school's basic educational philosophy as expressed in the mission statement serves citizenship education. The school's declaration of values and beliefs about the education of its pupils will need to be reviewed since citizenship education is about the promotion of values.

Citizenship education was previously one of the eight cross-curricular elements introduced in 1990 into the National Curriculum Council's publication *Curriculum Guidance*. It was characterised by a number of hallmarks which suggested that it had failed to address the problems it had been introduced to resolve. Among these were found the following: it was a non-assessment pursuit which had been taught largely by non-specialist teachers and delivered through personal and social education; its content was seldom made explicit and teachers were often left to divine it from what had been implied; there was also a lack of consistency in provision, with, at the more negative end, resistance to it from subject staff and little use being made of the wider community; it was found that such a lack of enthusiasm had filtered down to the pupils who viewed it as a low-status endeavour which had to be endured rather than enjoyed; the end 'result' was that pupils were unable to understand the connections between citizenship and their own individual subject, or indeed, more general aspects of the curriculum. The situation was bleak for citizenship education in many schools as it had relied upon being integrated into existing subjects of the curriculum, but this clearly had not been effective.

As citizenship education is now a National Curriculum subject in its own right it needs to be 'timetabled' in and outside of the school. Citizenship education should be a visible feature of the curriculum in every school which will require some specialist teaching with a specific content. Since it will be inspected, it will also need to be assessed, which in itself will raise the subject's status and give some consistency of provision in the long term. As a result of the importance of the area it may be that schools will appoint a senior member of staff to oversee its implementation and to examine the constraints and opportunities within which a school citizenship education policy can be formulated. This would also provide a good opportunity to involve less senior members of staff in the process and thus in turn be used as a vehicle for contributing towards their professional development. Qualities and skills such a senior coordinator would need are examined below.

Citizenship coordinator

A senior coordinator should demonstrate:

- experience of managing curriculum change;
- leadership qualities that provide for positive direction and leadership by example;
- management, organisational, motivational, planning and mentoring skills;
- credibility and interpersonal relationship skills and the ability to represent the subject with external agencies;
- ability to encourage team-work and participatory decision making among staff and the involvement of pupils in planning;
- ability to write a policy statement on citizenship education and create the atmosphere in which others can reflect and debate on it;
- ability to secure adequate school resources; and
- ability to select and deploy teaching staff to deliver citizenship education and to address such conflict and resistance that may arise.

Whoever is given responsibility for citizenship education will need the support and cooperation of the senior management of the school, have a supportive school ethos, a sympathetic staff and resources. A team or collaborative approach is also important and the coordinator could establish a working party. Such a team could generate new ideas and be creative in finding solutions through problem-solving exercises. As they work on how to implement citizenship education, an audit of current provision could be undertaken and recommendations for priorities in implementation made. This will provide staff with opportunities to initiate new ideas. Staff development in citizenship is another consideration which needs addressing by the senior management, but this will depend largely on the approach adopted by the school. Each school will reflect on the strengths and weaknesses of its existing curriculum as a starting point for the introduction of citizenship education, in an attempt to develop an informed yet critical view of citizenship education. This chapter will explore three basic approaches to citizenship education. Three basic possibilities have been selected since it would be impossible in a book of this nature to

cover the many variations in the planning and delivery of citizenship education. The three approaches are, then:

a) citizenship through the subject curriculum;
b) citizenship through or as a school subject; and
c) citizenship through the whole school.

Like many others involved with citizenship education it is our opinion that the most effective approach is the last. This, we believe, provides total exposure to citizenship across the curriculum and thus allows the most meaningful education for pupils.

Citizenship through the subject curriculum

If the purpose of education in England is to shape good members of society or, more precisely, good citizens, then some teachers might argue that the individual subjects of the curriculum already address the requirements set out in the Citizenship Order. This, to a certain extent, is true and finds its official expression in New Labour's Statement of Values, Aims and Purposes of the National Curriculum, published in 1999. Here it is argued that: 'Education influences and reflects the values of society, and the kind of society we want to be. It is important, therefore, to recognise a broad set of common values and purposes that underpin the school curriculum and the work of schools' (DfEE/QCA 1999: 10). The statement proceeds to list a number of qualities which should develop the 'well-being' of pupils and which should help them to become active citizens. In planning the school curriculum, the statement suggests that schools may wish to take account of the statement of values produced by the National Forum of Values in Education and the Community (QCA May 1998). This Forum produced a non-prescriptive framework for development that included four identified areas: the self, relationships, society and the environment. Effectively, the DfEE statement is a set of aims, values and purposes for citizenship education to which every school curriculum, and therefore every school subject, must contribute. It represents a growing concern to promote shared values and lists them as respect for self, others, society and environment.

There are of course particular aspects of individual subjects which already address and reflect these concerns in practice. The need to develop the spiritual and moral understanding of pupils, for example, is an explicit aim of all individual subjects and forms part of the assessment criteria inspected by OFSTED. Apart from the difference in terminology there is little to choose between this and the new requirement in citizenship education, as expressed by the advisory group, to develop the social and moral responsibility of pupils. Opportunities to become involved in the local, national and international community as well as an awareness of contemporary political issues can all be in part covered by existing practice within individual subjects. Yet although there already exist aims, content and methods inherent in the individual subjects of the current curriculum that develop good members of society, what is now hoped for is a greater teaching emphasis on the way in which active citizenship can be promoted. In this sense it is hoped that citizenship will not only support existing practice in the teaching of individual subjects but will also add a unique flavour to them. This can be achieved through linking the content of the citizenship order to the particular subject content that is relevant to it. This is effectively a cross-curricular approach not an inter-disciplinary approach which would be combinations of subjects such as 'integrated science' or 'humanities'. Cross-curricular can have different meanings, but essentially it is about planned collaboration between subjects. What, then, are the aspects inherent in the individual subjects of the current curriculum that already contribute to the shaping of good citizens?

The list of suggestions below is by no means exhaustive and it is not suggested that all subjects will be able to promote citizenship education to the same degree. Each subject area will need to decide which suggestions are appropriate for their curriculum and which can be developed with pupils of a particular age. Each subject department will no doubt consider and review the aims of their subject in the light of both the aims of the National Curriculum and the Citizenship Order and perhaps give greater emphasis to the kinds of opportunities described below.

Art

Art provides opportunities for pupils to:

- appreciate the work of others and understand the world through visual experience;
- recognise ideas of right and wrong in paintings;
- develop their own mode of expression;
- understand the cultural achievements of other people and societies;
- explore the diverse ways that artists working in different cultures produce images, symbols and objects.

Business and vocational education

Business and vocational education provide opportunities for pupils to:

- reflect on the choices available to them about work and leisure and consequences of such choices;
- analyse and understand alternative and different lifestyles and employment priorities;
- improve the community through an understanding of employment as service to others;
- understand their human and statutory rights as employees;
- develop a notion of a worthwhile job in society;

- seek consensus and the ability to negotiate and compromise with others; and
- work within teams and foster the well-being of the group.

Craft, design and technology

Craft, design and technology provides opportunities for pupils to:

- discuss the design of environmentally safe technology;
- understand the consequences of technological advancement for society;
- consider the underlying values and morality of the use of certain technologies;
- recognise the social impact of markets and goods;
- understand the needs of individuals and groups from different backgrounds in product design; and
- explore the political conflicts between the technological needs of individuals and groups.

Drama

Drama provides opportunities for pupils to:

- collaborate and cooperate with others in performance;
- understand and tolerate the points of view of others through role play;
- examine and explore relationships within community; and
- discover how they relate and fit in within their own community and society.

English

English provides opportunities for pupils to:

- understand the views , beliefs, opinions and feelings of others;
- express their own views, beliefs and opinions in an appropriate style;
- develop a sense of right and wrong by exploring the experiences of others;
- understand the sociability of human nature;
- understand and take account of audience and context;
- read how literature treats moral and political themes; and
- understand how literature contributes to the creation of a cultural identity.

Geography

Geography provides opportunities for pupils to:

- develop moral and ethical awareness in issues of equality, people, gender, race, culture and opportunities;
- understand cultural diversity and exercise respect and empathy for other peoples and societies;
- understand how societies work and appreciate our global interdependence and our need for sustainable development;
- experience field work outside of school to appreciate the physical and social context of communities;
- evaluate the consequences of actions for people, places and environments;
- understand the reasons for large-scale human migration; and
- explain and interpret social events among people and evaluate the political claims they make.

History

History provides opportunities for pupils to:

- broaden their experience of different peoples and cultures and appreciate the pluralist nature of our society;
- understand how values and human rights emerge within a society;
- analyse a variety of societal perspectives at both national and international levels;
- discuss the validity of evidence, motivations and opinions of people in different social, economic and political contexts;
- develop the ability to make value judgements and be familiar with the moral aspects of studying history;
- learn about the development of British democratic processes; and
- trace the development of citizens rights.

Information, communication and technology (ICT)

Information, communication and technology provides opportunities for pupils to:

- broaden their understanding of the global perspective; and
- link technology and its value to different ways of life.

Mathematics

Mathematics provides opportunities for pupils to:

* use logic in seeking proof for answers;
* compile, analyse and interpret statistical data, especially that relating to electoral systems and opinion polls; and
* use mathematics to solve real-life problems.

Music

Music provides opportunities for pupils to:

* experience emotion and a moral purpose;
* enjoy an expressive art within a social context; and
* develop the social skill of listening.

Modern languages

Modern languages provides opportunities for pupils to:

* learn social interaction in a new medium;
* study different cultures and lifestyles;
* explore alternative perspectives; and
* compare our society with different states in Europe, especially their institutions and political systems.

Personal, social and moral education

Personal, social and moral education (PSME) provides opportunities for pupils to:

* experience a range of different value perspectives on society and ethical issues;
* develop strategies for community involvement and service learning;
* enhance personal dispositions and positive attitudes; and
* understand the importance of tolerance and respect for others in a pluralist society.

Physical education

Physical education provides opportunities for pupils to:
* participate in games and teamwork which enhance collaboration and sociability;
* work together for cooperation and responsibility;

- become aware of the importance of their health and the health of others; and
- develop personal and group initiatives.

Religious education

Religious education provides opportunities for pupils to:

- understand the idea of duty and responsibility;
- develop positive relationships and friendships;
- explore the meaning of conflict;
- broaden their self-awareness and knowledge;
- enhance their potential for membership of strong communities; and
- understand the importance of shared values within community.

Science

Science provides opportunities for pupils to:

- understand the benefits and drawbacks of scientific development for society;
- discuss and consider the ethical considerations in science, such as medical ethics, genetic engineering and the environment; and
- understand life processes as they relate to human beings such as the promotion of health.

There are a number of obstacles to this 'citizenship through subject' approach, one of which is that the links between citizenship and the traditional subjects of the curriculum can appear tenuous. Another problem is the nature of the subjects themselves. Each National Curriculum subject is well established and has broad areas of consensus on the way it should be taught and what might be expected from the pupil. There are often common understandings of the nature of teaching and learning in subjects and the teachers develop a shared language of the subject and even depend on progression in it for career development. There is therefore a subject subculture and much of these subjects are 'givens' that are already purposes, aims and values in the National Curriculum. This can act as an obstacle to the introduction of citizenship education and can present unconscious resistance from subject teachers who become unable to deliver it through integration with their subject, but continually see it as something 'extra'. In the worst-case scenario, citizenship would become a peripheral inconvenience in the subject. It is also hard to monitor and the visibility of the subject may disappear. Overall responsibility for the area may be absolved under such circumstances.

Although all subjects of the curriculum will be expected to contribute to the teaching of citizenship, English, history and geography in particular have been singled out as providing a distinctive contribution to its promotion. This came about as a result of the Advisory Group's theory that the content and intended learning outcomes of citizenship education overlap most significantly with these subjects. As a result, aspects of the Citizenship Order have been inserted into the individual programmes of study for English, history and geography and will in effect form part of them. These 'citizenship insertions' will ensure that the content of some lessons in the subject is guided to comply with the imperatives of the Citizenship Order. What this means in practice is effectively a 'two-birds-with-one-stone' approach: when addressing the nature of the Stalinist state in the Soviet Union, or the Holocaust, for example, teachers will simultaneously be addressing and emphasising the need stated in the Citizenship Order to teach the 'legal and human rights and responsibilities underpinning society'. Many schools will no doubt simply adjust the content of PSHE to include strands of citizenship education within it, but the complexities involved in teaching citizenship through PSHE will need to be recognised. One teacher cannot teach the range of subject areas that will be required.

Citizenship through or as a school subject

Citizenship education can and will be taught as a distinct subject on the curriculum in many schools. It may appear as a distinct element within personal and social education or stand alone as a timetabled subject. As part of personal and social education it has the advantage of possibly being person centred, group orientated and based on a partnership between teacher and pupil which emphasises experiential learning and a movement away from didactic teaching. However, it may lack any distinctive content in this arrangement. What the content of this citizenship education will be and who teaches it will vary from school to school, but additional content is necessary, for the main subjects of the curriculum do not automatically cover the content of citizenship. There are some key concepts which are peculiar to citizenship which is one reason for removing it from personal and social education and giving it its own timetabled slot. Once a person has been identified as the coordinator of this area it is important to decide what is to be taught. This can only be achieved after it is known what is already taught through the school ethos and formal and informal curriculum. In planning the curriculum for citizenship education you first need to begin with the programmes of study in the Citizenship Order, but these need to be described and interpreted. One way to describe and understand the content of citizenship education is to view the subject as comprising a set of concepts, dispositions and experiences which are to be promoted. The following provides some indication of the aims of such a programme and in each area it is assumed that the teacher might begin with the local community and build up to the national and international perspectives. It is also assumed that a citizenship vocabulary would be gradually introduced so that concepts necessary to construct a conceptual framework – order, justice, law, representation, freedom, welfare, etc. – are established and addressed.

The aims of citizenship education must seek to understand the democratic principles, values and practices including the historical development of English democracy as well as the role and function of the law. Individual and group participation in socio-political offices incorporating civil rights and responsibilities, socio-political action and democratic processes of change need to be studied and experienced in some way. It must also incorporate skills such as critical thinking, problem solving, personal–social participation skills necessary for effective living and knowledge of democracy. Learning about duties, responsibilities and rights is also a chief aim of citizenship education together with:

- the nature and structure of the community – local, national and international;
- the importance of active participative citizenship;
- knowledge of Britain's political system; and
- the interdependence of individuals and communities.

The emphasis is therefore on a specific content. In planning for citizenship education teachers need to build a framework for citizenship education which includes an understanding of the learner and society, aims and objectives, content selection, scope and sequence, modes of transaction and evaluation. As a consequence of this pupils need to have knowledge of and understand the following concepts.

Concepts in citizenship education

Social systems and structures

How are communities socially organised and structured, by whom, for whom and for what purpose? This would involve an analysis of the way in which 'the community' is made up of a variety of differing communities, such as the regional, the religious and the ethnic. It would also include an analysis of the way in which such communities are served and supported. This would involve a study of local democracy, councils and their departments together with a detailed look at public services such as social work, transport, financial systems (Council Tax) and the education system. This can then be extended to national policies and international structures. Alternative ways of governing the country would be considered such as the debate between centralised and devolved, or federal governments. Indeed, questions could be raised as to how far devolution or federalisation should go.

Decision making

How do people make decisions for the community in a democracy? A discussion of the process of decision making could begin with local elections and the party political system in Britain. The processes of representation could be explained together with why people seek election to office and the principles that they promote.

Power

How is power exercised and distributed within a democracy? Pupils will need to explore the meaning of power and understand the authority behind such power when it is exercised by police officers, courts of law and members of the public in various offices. They also need to understand the nature of the institutional checks and balances on the exercise or abuse of that power. This could include studying the significance of a free press and the role of the parliamentary opposition.

Change

How can the contribution of an individual make a difference in a democracy? This question relates to the forces of change and includes an understanding of the purposes of trade unions, companies, multinationals and international organisations, banks and pressure groups. It promotes how different means can be used to influence events in any community.

Conflict

How do we understand the nature and sources of conflict in society? This is concerned with the means through which conflicts are resolved and agreements are reached. It concerns a study of institutions that exist to resolve conflict such as Parliament and the courts.

Each of these concepts provide enormous scope for interpretation by the teacher and it is for the teacher to design an appropriate learning strategy to promote the desired learning outcomes.

Dispositions

Dispositions will include all the attitudes, skills, values and virtues which the school deems desirable and worth promoting. In this area the whole school is responsible for their promotion and they include among others basic skills in communication, listening to others, problem solving, organising, planning, analysing, assessing, debating, finding out and making choices in life. They are also concerned with critical awareness and thinking. However, within a distinct citizenship education course some particular dispositions, values and attitudes might be particularly promoted. These include:

a) a concern for justice, equality and fairness;
b) an interest in community affairs;
c) an understanding of human rights;
d) cultivation of a sense of duty and responsibility to neighbours;

e) understanding the needs of others;

f) an appreciation of inter-dependence at all levels;

g) the development of individual empowerment;

h) a recognition of the importance of freedom and truth; and

i) the ability and desire to participate in the life of the school and wider community.

Experiences

Citizenship education is about action and participation so pupils, therefore, need structured experiences which the school culture and ethos already offer them. Are pupils free to express views in the classroom? Do they have sufficient opportunities in their learning to cooperate with each other? Are they consulted about changes in the school? Is there a school council? These are the type of questions which need to be addressed when citizenship education is being developed or introduced for the first time to the school. Other experiences may consist of a range of extra-curricular activities:

a) field trips and outdoor education;

b) residential visits;

c) visits abroad;

d) clubs and societies;

e) community involvement;

f) charity activities for the wider community;

g) work experience placements; and

h) school councils.

All of these areas can be important elements within the citizenship education curriculum.

Citizenship through the whole school

The curriculum in an English school consists of the following elements set within a school ethos: religious education, subjects – both core and foundation, a range of cross-curricular elements and extra-curricular activities. The success of any school will depend on whether or not it has a common vision and a climate conducive to learning. The success of citizenship education will also depend on the importance given to a whole-school approach. It must be seen as lifelong development to which many other experiences outside of school will contribute. In this each pupil has a unique starting point and we need to respect each pupil's needs so that we understand that there will naturally be different outcomes. The kind of school ethos operating will have a significant influence on the type of characters or even citizens that the school is nurturing. Citizenship education is learnt and cultivated in part through the school ethos which is the context for the development of worthwhile values. It is the school ethos which will infuse all other aspects of a school's life and work and so the question of how a school develops an ethos which helps pupils participate in democratic processes needs to be addressed. There are a number of contexts which contribute to citizenship education; these include parental influence, the school and the wider community. Therefore it is essential that any coherent whole-school policy on citizenship involves as many people as possible in deciding what needs to be done to implement citizenship education. One starting point could be to discern whether or not a school has a positive ethos in displaying the following characteristics:

a) a good atmosphere or spirit within the school community which celebrates individual and collective success;

b) shared aims and values which are promoted in the school culture;

c) an attractive environment conducive to learning;

d) high and consistent expectations, both at academic and pastoral levels;

e) participation of the pupils in the life of the school through formal and informal structures;

f) an emphasis on learning and positive staff attitudes to pupils;

g) extra-curricula activities which broaden pupils' interests and experiences;

h) responsibility being shared by pupils and positive pupil attitudes to teachers;

i) a recognition of individual and collective needs;

j) a collaborative approach to teaching and learning;

k) a respect for the rights of pupils with a just system of rewards and sanctions;

l) a holistic view of education;

m) links with the wider community as an essential feature which encourages a warm welcome to visitors to the school;

n) a strong sense of school community and a good pastoral system which helps pupils feel that they belong; and

o) democratic forms of school governance in which staff are involved in the decision-making processes.

Citizenship education is reflected and promoted within the whole life and ethos of the school and is an essential backdrop to teaching citizenship education effectively. The school is a micro-community and how it is run and the relationships between teachers and pupils will have a significant influence on citizenship education. Whole-school events such as mock elections or 'Democracy Days' (Davies 1999), the establishment of school councils, international exchange programmes, community projects for the elderly and disabled, links with industry, visits to theatres and cinema, the development of skills to participate actively in society, and charity work are all part of building a healthy school ethos. A whole-school approach will also involve permeation of citizenship into all subjects, but it requires a great deal of coordination, liaison and planning.

A whole-school approach to delivering citizenship can also be facilitated by adopting a modular structure. This has the advantage of involving a great many staff and can be designed in a number of flexible ways. It also has the advantage of being presented as discrete blocks of activity, or mini-courses with no previous experience necessary to study it. A module is capable of being taken at any time and can be a stand alone course or part of a mainstream course or even concerned with the development of skills or planned learning experiences. Choice and flexibility are central to such an approach and these can build on pupil interests as well as their strengths. Ideas can be piloted in curriculum experiments and this provides a change in pace for the school. Modules can be directed to community involvement and can be activity weeks. Each module can have a short-term goal with a clear objective for achievement in mind, with the development of cooperation in a team as an important by-product of them. The whole approach depends on how flexible the teaching arrangements are in the school. Overall, a whole-school approach will consist of developing a strong positive ethos, ensuring strong cross-curricular provision combined with discrete elements of citizenship education recognisable as a subject on the timetabled curriculum. Putting it into practice will also require an action plan. In this teachers will need to address the following:

- priorities;
- time scales;
- who is involved;
- how it will be done; and
- success criteria.

The importance of citizenship on the way schools are governed is vital (Deem, Brehony and Heath 1995). Some believe that we can teach citizenship education entirely from a skills-based approach. While skills development is an essential element of teaching citizenship education there also needs to be included the links made between the different concepts in citizenship as well as the development of dispositions of good citizenship.

Conclusion

Citizenship education is not a matter of accruing information. It heralds changes for schools in ethos, aims, management structures and teaching and learning. It can open up the curriculum and get teachers to talk and collaborate in their planning of the curriculum. Space must be provided for planning and the reasons for the curriculum approach adopted need to be clearly articulated and owned by the staff. Teachers will need to define the content, organise the knowledge for teaching and sequence it. It will still require a cross-curricular collaboration. Citizenship education is premised on active, experiential learning and it has a socially transforming potential for society. What is planned must be achievable and the hidden curriculum also needs to be addressed. Some will recognise that citizenship education should be a subject taught by specially trained teachers and that citizenship as a subject will be easier to manage and deliver out of the classroom. However, this implementation will need to be phased in over a period of time. An essential part in achieving this is ensuring that there is a sense among the staff that its implementation is collectively owned by them.

Tasks

TASK 2.1

Producing a whole-school policy for citizenship education

A school's policy and practice on citizenship education needs to be set in the wider context of the school's overall aims, culture, ethos and values and its concern for the development of the whole child. What would a comprehensive policy for your school include? Reflect on and articulate your own school's values as they apply to citizenship education. Identify what practices need to be changed in your school in order to achieve the desired goals of citizenship education.

TASK 2.2

Skills for effective citizenship

The kinds of skills that are necessary to cultivate a 'good citizen' can be found and promoted through the subjects of the National Curriculum. Consider the 'skills' for citizenship listed below and identify how your own subject already contributes to the development of them:

- knowing how to plan, organise and debate;
- recognising bias and distortion in evidence and arguments;
- distinguishing between fact and opinion;
- understanding that choices have consequences for oneself and others;
- having the ability to evaluate alternative viewpoints;
- examining sources in a critical and analytical way;
- interpreting data and understanding the reasoning and justification of others;
- developing an ability to listen, negotiate and compromise;
- having the ability to handle data and work with others; and
- having the ability to evaluate personal decisions.

CHAPTER 3

Implementing citizenship education: A curriculum case study

Ian Potter

Introduction

This chapter is about one school's approach to citizenship education.

Objectives

By the end of this chapter you should:

* understand our reasons for taking the approach outlined;
* have a good idea of our approach to citizenship education;
* be appraised of some of the issues in taking such an approach; and
* be able to reflect upon whether such an approach is applicable to your school and circumstances.

Our school is an LEA-maintained 12–18 mixed comprehensive school. It serves a partially rural catchment area and is housed in modern buildings. Since the school opened in 1963 it has grown to a current size of 1800 students. With over 100 teaching staff and nearly as many again in support and service capacities we are a sizeable and significant community. We are an organisation of approximately 2000 people working within a defined area for a large proportion of the day.

We have been awarded Beacon school status following a successful OFSTED inspection. Our strength is in being a truly comprehensive school adding considerable value to the range of students we teach. The testing we carry out on entry to the school demonstrates our intake is in line with the national average. Our results at GCSE and Post 16 are significantly higher than national averages. We have only a low percentage on free school meals and acknowledge that the majority of our students do not face the socio-economic difficulties experienced by some other school populations. This, however, is not to deny the challenges and personal circumstances faced by many of our students, and their respective needs.

Today, with corporate downsizing, decentralisation and 'hot-desking', there are not many organisations, apart from large schools, prisons and possibly hospitals, with large resident populations. To manage and lead such a diverse group of people 'under-one-roof', as exists in a large school, is extremely demanding. Generating a sense of community is an important leadership function, as well as recognising the ever more demanding relationship between the school community and the community it serves – not to mention government expectations! It should not, therefore, be a surprise to the reader that at our school we take seriously notions of citizenship and ways in which our populations can successfully find ways to work with each other to the benefit of all our members.

We state the aims of the school in the following way:

Valuing all students we believe in the active promotion of equal opportunities for all and work:

To provide the knowledge and skills our students need in order to:

- develop as well-balanced people;
- make full and positive contributions to our society; and
- succeed in an increasingly technological and international environment.

To develop in our students positive values and attitudes:

- fairness and justice;
- tolerance;
- respect for others;
- honesty;
- cooperation;
- loyalty;
- enjoyment of and commitment to learning;
- independence;
- personal responsibility;
- courtesy and consideration;
- self-confidence; and
- flexibility.

To encourage and help all students to achieve their best.

The school has tried to make these aims a reality through its policies and practice. In particular, our curriculum policy places considerable emphasis on the personal and social development and education of our students. We have a holistic view with regard to the education of children and are clear about it being the responsibility of every teacher, within their lessons, to be mindful about the development of the whole person. We expect teachers, where it is appropriate, to having learning objectives within any of their lessons that relate to the personal and social education of students. Our school development plan maintains initiatives aimed at developing further the aspects of school life that contribute to what many call the 'hidden' curriculum. We take a view that the majority of what we do and say in school, and the quality of relationships and communications, are instrumental in the culture we create and the standards we achieve. Hence, it is not a problem to embrace the subject of citizenship, so long as we do so within an integrated approach. The argument for such an approach now follows.

The argument

The National Curriculum Order for citizenship emphasises that 'teaching should ensure that knowledge and understanding about becoming informed citizens are acquired and applied when developing skills of enquiry and communication, and participation and responsible action'. This has been paraphrased, earlier in this book, as the Order maintaining 'that knowledge about citizenship is best acquired through the skills of citizenship'. Our interpretation would be one related to the concept of experiential learning.

At Ousedale School, we have taken the view that good citizenship education is one in which knowledge is best learnt and understood within an applied context. Students make best sense of the content of the Citizenship Order when they are learning about it in a 'real' context. Learning is at its optimum when students can relate to the subject matter, hence the use of the term 'real'. Learning is real for a learner if they can relate to the matter in hand.

Some teenagers, probably the majority, are well-behaved conformists who will go through the motions of learning in schools without really valuing what they are doing or believing in the sense of it. They respond obediently to the teaching methods used and make what sense they can out of that which is 'delivered'. What they learn in such a context will never be as good as that which they learn in a lesson that has relevance and purpose for them.

There are also teenagers who are less conformist and will be far less polite in their response to the teaching of a subject that seems to them a distance away from what they need and want from school. It is an easy point to make that these are the very students to whom we should be reaching in achieving their understanding and acquisition of the skills of citizenship. The important point is that to engender an academic profile to the subject of citizenship will fail even more to reach such students. It is already a fault of much of what we do in secondary schools, that we alienate many of our students by 'academicising' learning. It is understandable that we as providers of education (teachers, government officers, possibly ministers, politicians and civil servants) have developed our self-esteem and self-concept around our academic profile, and we wish to perpetuate its worth through the value we place on it within our schools. To do so with citizenship education would be to miss the point as to its purpose, misunderstand the essence of the Crick Report and fail to keep the emphasis of the order as outlined and interpreted above.

Teaching is a creative process because it continually has to experiment, explore and find ways of motivating the learners. Whether this makes it more of an art or a science is less important than realising that it is most definitely about helping the learner come to their own understanding. This they will do if it falls within their 'frame of reference', alternatively expressed as within their experience. An adolescent, like any one, will work hard to achieve if they can see the value in doing so; if what is presented to them fits with their experience and the construct of the world in which they live.

There is an assumption underpinning this argument. It is that if we are to teach citizenship, then it is to be done effectively and in the best way we can, within our particular circumstances. Having established a commitment to the ideals of citizenship education, the question a school must address is how to introduce or develop it further within their curriculum in a way that will be relevant and 'meaningful' to their students. How do you organise the teaching of citizenship so that your teenagers will value it, and therefore learn from it and enable you to feel you have fulfilled your commitment? In fact, how does one organise any subject in school to motivate students to achieve in it? The answer given by many is 'to accredit it'.

There is a real convenience to this answer. It avoids tackling issues of intrinsic worth by making them self-evident in the carrot-on-the-end-of-a-stick approach of extrinsic gain. Learners are motivated not by the value of the subject itself, but by what it can provide for them. Is this the essence of citizenship? It may in a sense be true to say that the real reason for being an informed citizen practising good citizenship is that one will feel better about oneself, and possibly do better in life (subject to criteria chosen). Yet, we would argue that the proper purpose of citizenship education should be to prevent a selfishly driven society and to work towards one in which citizens understand and are aware of their responsibilities to each other. Thus, to make citizenship the subject of accreditation may be to undermine our preferred objective.

In one sense, however, at Ousedale, we have 'capitalised' on the examination gravy train, but by turning around the usual argument. In considering the assumption that students are motivated by the extrinsic gain of examination grades, where better to locate the teaching of citizenship than within their examination subjects? This is particularly relevant at Key Stage 4 where students have had a choice about doing a significant number of the subjects. Students also appreciate the importance of the core NC subjects in providing them future opportunity, and so if success in these is related to the fulfilling of the Citizenship Orders, they may be more likely to value the work involved in citizenship education.

On a more serious note, however, the real reasons for linking the teaching of examination subjects with the Citizenship Orders are in line with the arguments outlined above. Namely:

- Citizenship education is most effective when learnt in a relevant context.
- If the understanding and acquisition of the skills and knowledge of citizenship are best achieved through some form of experiential learning, then so too would the understanding and knowledge of most, if not all, subjects. An integration of citizenship education with the teaching of say English, maths, science, etc. would enhance the learning of those subjects as well.
- An integration approach gives a school the opportunity to re-look at its pedagogy and how students learn best.
- Such an approach revisits with teachers the purpose of students learning their particular subject. This is especially significant at secondary level where all too often teachers promote their subject in terms of learners studying it to the highest level, instead of promoting the purpose of the subject being to enable all students to understand themselves and the world around them better.
- A whole school approach to citizenship teaching provides a curriculum and staff development opportunity in which a greater sense of learning coherence and continuity can be sought.
- Teachers who perceive their role in an isolated way are encouraged to widen their perception and appreciate more how the way they teach can influence the sense that a student makes from his or her whole-school experience.
- Students learn through the integrated approach that there are many transferable aspects, skills and knowledge from one subject to another. The making of these connections can help raise achievement.

There is something circular about the justification, for which we make no apology. An integrated approach to the teaching of citizenship, if effectively introduced and implemented, will raise standards within the school. These are not only academic and examination standards, but also standards of personal, social, moral behaviour. The ethos and/or culture of the school will improve.

Our argument is supported by the Order itself, as explained in chapter one: 'The order also sets out the way in which education *about* citizenship is attained as a result of education *through* citizenship.... This ensures that teaching and learning methods focus on the active as opposed to what had previously been more passive methods of simply acquiring knowledge' (my italics). Moreover, readers will also recall the following words from that chapter: 'Social and moral education are clearly a prerequisite for and essential requirements of citizenship education... social and moral dimensions of citizenship education are not simply about knowledge or learning rules, but must be experienced and indeed lived'.

Our school approach

The previous chapter stated:

> Whole-school events such as mock elections or 'Democracy Days' (Davies 1999), the establishment of school councils, ... development of skills to participate actively in society, and charity work are all part of building a healthy school ethos. A whole-school approach will also involve permeation of citizenship into all subjects, but it requires a great deal of coordination, liaison and planning. We would argue that good schools are already doing many if not all of the activities listed in the fuller quotation. It should not need citizenship to become a NC subject for such things to happen. It does probably, however, require the legislation to bring about the 'permeation of citizenship into all subjects'.

The point may need reiterating that schools will only prioritise the energy to plan, coordinate and monitor the implementation of citizenship education if they think it important. Only time will tell whether, by making it law, schools have taken a committed approach, or a tokenistic one in response to what they perceived as a top-down initiative. Our feeling would be that successful schools are able to use external agendas to their own advantage and gain. Citizenship education, therefore, can be seen in a similar way to that of PSE, literacy, numeracy and ICT.

Discrete subject teachers are becoming more comfortable with the idea that in order to improve learning in their own subject area they have a responsibility for the development of literacy and numeracy skills *within* their area of the curriculum. It is rare nowadays to hear a teacher of (for example) history talk about an absolution of responsibility for the literacy skills of the students in his or her class. (Well, not too loudly anyway!) Most teachers recognise that it is no longer just the 'job of the English and maths teacher', but that something like literacy and numeracy has to be coordinated in a whole-school way. These are not bound by discrete subject identity. They are by their very nature cross-curricula and are taught most effectively within a balance of discrete skill input and the applied context.

Information, communication and technology can be added to the list of learning skills that all teachers must embrace if their teaching is to be effective. This is happening as they realise its benefits and become more confident themselves. In one sense, it is easier with ICT because there has never been a traditional subject upon which non-ICT teachers have relied. As a result, there is less change needed to expect all teachers to develop teaching skills that take account of ICT and its advantages for enhancing students' learning. Most staff see the influence ICT is having in their own as well as the students' lives, and so are fairly accepting of its inclusion within their own classroom practice. Why was it then that when it is so obvious that literacy and numeracy skills are so vital to their own lives and those around them, there was a sense of denial by many teachers of their responsibility for developing such skills in their own classrooms? Perhaps it has something to do with the point made earlier about the 'academic' industry and the promotion of the forms of knowledge around which so many have constructed their self-identity.

Our school has added the teaching of PSE to this list of aspects that are becoming more recognisable by teachers of whatever subject as part of their responsibility. We intend to do the same for Citizenship. We joke that perhaps one day we might advertise for 'a teacher of literacy, numeracy, thinking skills, PSE, health, guidance, and citizenship, teaching within the science department to GCSE and advanced level examinations in chemistry'. The implementation of citizenship, if approached in the way we advocate, is a broader process than that usually associated with curriculum development. It is more about changing the culture of the school. There is much literature about the management of change and school improvement, and undoubtedly some of that has influenced us. The key principle to our approach has been 'the making use of an external requirement to meet the aims of our school'. It is the job of senior management to *re-present* initiatives from external agencies in such a way that they 'feel' like something that would fit within the school. This is not 'selling-out' on what one believes in, nor indeed is it an act of compromise. It is in fact accommodation. It is the taking of a pragmatic approach in order to maintain recognition of your ideals. Citizenship education is a really positive example.

The statutory nature of citizenship at Key Stages 3 and 4 presents itself as an external 'stick' onto which all sorts of negative, sceptical and even cynical meanings could be attached. There are teachers who are wary of the social engineering implications of teaching children how to be 'proper' citizens. They have also serious concerns about some teachers taking advantage of such a subject as 'citizenship' to promote their own value systems. Others question whether the objectives of such a 'subject' can cater sufficiently and appropriately for the diversity and range within our multicultural society. There is the continual fear that schools are being expected to make up for the shortfalls of other agencies of socialisation and rather than embrace the initiative, teachers should take the opportunity to state clearly where their responsibility ends. The educational establishment should argue for clarity about the purposes of schooling in today's society. All this, plus complaints about the 'quart-into-pint-pot' syndrome of the National Curriculum.

In introducing citizenship education into a school, allowance must be made for these areas of concern to be aired. There would be a degree of shallowness in the organisation if on the one hand students were in their citizenship lessons being encouraged to question and understand the workings of society, its power structures and systems of justice, and on the other hand the staff were not! Our discussions *range* around the following points (please note the present tense; it does, and should, remain a talking point):

- The propaganda issue about the state or an individual imposing their values should never go away. It is a healthy debate in any liberal society, especially one purporting to be a democracy. We have included reference to the 'Statement of Values by the

National Forum for Values in Education and the Community' in our discussions. This is a statement that appears in National Curriculum documentation. A quotation: 'Agreement on these values is compatible with different interpretations and applications of them. It is for schools to decide, reflecting on the range of views in the wider community, how these values should be interpreted and applied.' There seems to be the implication that the statement of values is itself relative to the context of a school. If this is disconcerting to the reader, this further quote may relieve your discomfort: 'Schools and teachers can have confidence that there is general agreement in society upon these values. They therefore can expect the support and encouragement of society if they base their teaching and school ethos on these values.' These words have hopefully brought comfort to those worried about not getting right the values underpinning their school and lessons!

• More seriously, however, our discussions have centred around a commitment to do 'right' by our children and their community. This has inevitably led to consideration of the context in which we are working but also placing our situation within the wider context of our regional, national and international responsibilities. This is where the Statement of Values did have some true worth existing alongside our own school aims. Our commitment to do the best for our children leads us to 'accommodate' their needs beyond those which are academic. If one's concept of learning is more to do with 'life-skills' than with the narrower perception of the 'application of knowledge', then by definition a learning organisation will take on board responsibilities wider than those purely required for schooling young people. It is not the fault of the child if there is a lacking in society's structures to address her needs.

• While we agonise about society's failings and refuse to do anything in case we set a precedent, the children continue to lose out. It may well be defeatist to resign ourselves to the notion that we will end up having to teach citizenship anyway, so let us get started. Likewise, it may be short-termist not to force a more strategic debate and solution to the problem... but coming back to the children of *now*, they have only this one chance. When we didn't know, we had an excuse for not doing our best, but when we do, do we have an excuse? Is resistance valid as far as those children and their community are concerned?

• Finding 'time' to do all this is a riddle worthy of a sphinx. The answer, as with any *real* question, is not a simple one. If it has to be done then a way has to be 'found'. The cliché about finding time is true, and it is done by having clarity about that which you value the most. Schools that spend time on getting academic results at the expense of the 'culture', are wasting their time. Schools that deny the investment required in meeting the personal, social, cultural, moral and spiritual needs of their children will not be making most effective use of their time. If their results are good then they are not achieving them in the most efficient way because if those schools were to have their priorities in better focus, then their results would be better. It is a matter, once again, of values.

It seems that whenever you start something new you are supposed to carry out an audit! To a large extent, this makes sense. It is probably necessary to be clear about where you are at present, if anything to avoid doing more than you have to! Also to ensure the picture you think you have of what is going on is actually accurate. Yet we all know that many audits do not present a true illustration because their findings are dependent on the honesty and quality of the answers, and more significantly on the questions that were asked. An audit can only provide information about that which it measures.

As demonstrated in the last section, it is important to have an idea, and ideally some sort of measure, of where the staff 'stand' on citizenship. What are their attitudes, values and beliefs with regard to the Citizenship Order?

It may, however, be advisable first to ask staff to make comments based on their initial impressions of Citizenship Education. This would allow an airing of the concerns discussed earlier. A possible way of doing this, dependent on the size of the staff, is to get them to position themselves on a continuum between, at one extreme: 'Citizenship is a positive innovation for schools', to the other, 'I feel pretty hostile towards the introduction of citizenship'. This exercise could be done with all the staff together literally standing on a continuum marked out on the floor, or standing in front of a continuum marked out an a sheet of lining paper hanging on the wall. To make the exercise light-hearted, an outline of each person's head and shoulders could be drawn on to the paper (or feet in the case of the continuum being on the floor). The member of staff then writes their name within the head (or feet). Discussion as a whole staff, or in smaller groups, could then focus on why people had positioned themselves as they did. In larger schools it may be advisable to ensure that there are a spread of 'positions' represented within each group.

Following on from the above exercise, staff could be given a copy of the programmes of study for citizenship. 'From 2002, schools will have a statutory responsibility to teach the programmes of study for citizenship at key stages 3 and 4. The programmes of study set out what pupils should be taught in citizenship and provide the basis for planning schemes of work' (The National Curriculum for England 2000).

A further activity for staff would be to highlight what in the programmes of study they feel warm about and what leaves them feeling cold.

Again, discussion should ensue from this activity, but this time in curriculum-based groups. This is in order to facilitate the next stage of the auditing process. It is probable that secondary teachers from a similar subject area will have a greater degree of consensus about the citizenship programmes of study than a group of teachers from a diverse set of subjects. This assertion is based not only on experience but also on the observation that the citizenship document makes links to the programmes of study of other National Curriculum subjects. Putting aside the issue that teachers within the same department can have differing philosophies and values about the purpose of their teaching, it is a fairly safe assumption that greater commonality in approach can be found among teachers of a similar discipline, than from those of varied academic orientation. Hence, such discussion groups are likely to conclude in one or several of the following ways:

1. We cannot see what relevance the teaching of citizenship has in our subject area.
2. We feel the teaching of citizenship may have some relevance to the learning objectives in our subject, but are unable to see how we could, or should, include it in our subject area.
3. We can see that citizenship education would be of value in this school but we are not teachers of it. We've got enough to do!
4. To focus on citizenship education in our subject area would detract from what we have to do already. Give us some more time and maybe we could do it!
5. Though in principle we can see the value of citizenship education, we are concerned from which curriculum area the time is to be taken to teach it.
6. Quality not quantity is what counts. Yet we can see that citizenship has positive advantages for increasing a sense of relevance in our subject for students.
7. We suggest that the PSHE/careers lessons the school presently timetables are renamed citizenship. If not those, then what about the life skills and thinking skills lesson we run?
8. We are interested in the opportunities that certain aspects of the citizenship programmes of study may bring to our own existing schemes of work.
9. We think that we already do quite a bit of what is required by the programmes of study. We would need to focus our learning objectives and assessment intentions to ensure that we were teaching the orders as outlined.
10. We would like to change our job descriptions to become teachers of citizenship!

Staff are aware of the statutory nature of the citizenship programmes of study. They also know that the school curriculum is crowded. At a crude micro-political level, departments will need to consider their response in terms of responding to the Orders positively or separating themselves from them. To do the latter might be to alienate the department from any time or resources that will support the initiative.

In the light of these organisational implications (enforced by the statutory nature of the programmes of study) departments may agree to consider further the possible positive benefits of embracing citizenship. This is not as cynical as at first it may seem. It must be recognised that subject-centred teachers have not necessarily had the luxury of the time to think about the whys and wherefores of citizenship education. Almost certainly they will not come to the documentation with a mindset that celebrates the opportunities it presents. Rather, they will see it in terms of the change it necessitates. They will understandably take a view that it will require more work and therefore naturally resist it. This is where senior managers have to earn their money. And if transactional methods of leadership open the doors for more transformational styles of management, then so be it.

It would be naive to suggest that heads of department would all immediately buy into the idealistic integrationalist approach to citizenship education. The only context in which this might occur is in schools where practice has long been established that the teaching of transferable learning objectives, such as literacy, PSE, numeracy and study skills, has to be done in a cross-curricula way if it is to be truly effective. Where this is not the prevailing culture within a school it is not wrong for management to use allocation of time and resources as a way into the wider debate. This is so long as the more fundamental issues are explored and decisions are not made purely on the basis of expediency.

A strategy to get staff to think about the number of slices of the timetable cake that can be achieved with the introduction of this new National Curriculum subject is to compare the programmes of study for citizenship with those for music and/or art. It soon becomes apparent that there is not much difference in length between them. Obviously, this only refers to Key Stage 3 here, but is the logical development that the same time is allocated to the teaching of citizenship as to the teaching of music, or art? And then at Key Stage 4 (where interestingly, the programme of study for citizenship is longer than at Key Stage 3) should the time be the same as it was in Key Stage 3, or longer?

It is significant that the 5 per cent of curriculum time that was talked about at one point for citizenship is no longer discussed in such terms. This will be because as Professor Crick said 'Teachers and governors must be realising how different it [citizenship] is from other, more conventional subject orders. Citizenship is, in essence, a different type of national curriculum subject" and schools are being encouraged to decide on their own methods of accommodating the Orders within their curriculum. Five per cent, however, remains the recommendation for music! The audit now shifts from measuring people's disposition towards citizenship education towards what is already happening within the curriculum. *There is already in existence much good practice – we just don't recognise it as citizenship education.*

Our advice would be to identify what, in the orders, is already being 'covered'. The extent to which the requirements of citizenship education are currently in place probably won't be a surprise. What will be a pleasant discovery is the likelihood that little will in fact need to be implemented. This is only reassuring if one is thinking minimally and merely in terms of the statutory order, and not anticipating the catalyst effect that this new subject can have on school culture and improvement.

In the 'bigger picture' of the implementation of citizenship education, curriculum development is seen as more than programmes of study and schemes of work. Instead, the curriculum content is used as a vehicle for exploring pedagogy and classroom ethos. The implementation of citizenship is seen as an opportunity to reaffirm the type of practice we value most within the classroom and beyond. This new subject is a means by which to ask again 'what is our purpose within schools?' Such an approach transcends the letter of the order, and uses them as part of a wider agenda.

Ask most headteachers or senior managers what it is in their school that gets in the way of their organisation moving forward and improving and they will cite reasons and examples that are qualitative in their nature. They will talk about quality of relationships, staff room and management cultures, dominant behaviours in classrooms that have negative effects on learning and issues related to the ethos of the school. Hence, the argument that an approach to the implementation of citizenship that is intended to address the 'bigger picture' need not be perceived as yet another initiative but alternatively as something that will support the strategic direction of the school. In this way, the citizenship orders become part of the school development plan, not as an adjunct, but as a facilitator for school improvement. Curriculum development is synonymous with staff development, and is instrumental in moving the school forward.

Schools are the type of organisation in which change is probably more effective if it is incremental and evolutionary. This is because of the inherent tension within schools that learners need to feel safe in order to take the risk of the discomfort zone necessary for the most effective learning and change to occur. Another paradox is the inertia that naturally comes with the concern that for a given cohort of students this is their one chance and that any change had better be an improvement. Squaring the circle of the conflicting paradigms of conservatism and radical thinking requires creative leadership and staff to 'think outside of the box'. We would call it a process a re-conceptualisation.

Re-conceptualisation is about seeing what we do already in a different way. It is re-presenting to oneself the nature and purpose of the activity that one is re-conceptualising. For example, a teacher and student engaged in an activity that has learning goals related to a specific subject objective, such as in science, will re-conceptualise the value of that activity. They will start to see the point of the learning exercise in a different way. They will have a change in the frame of reference into which that activity fits. Expressed in a more concrete way, it means that teachers, and in turn students, will see that what was taught and learnt previously fulfilled certain subject-specific criteria. It now fulfils objectives related to citizenship education as well as the subject requirements. Their concept of the aim of the lesson has broadened to not only address aspects of the discrete National Curriculum subject, but also the Citizenship Order.

In the early stages of creating a citizenship curriculum the school should focus on the principle of taking what is presently done and re-conceptualising it within a citizenship education frame of reference. This is a far more exciting and challenging task than merely adding something into an already overcrowded curriculum. It will lead a school to consider seriously its whole curriculum framework. It will encourage curriculum managers to make connections between subject areas and facilitate students to transfer skills and knowledge from lesson to lesson in ways that they perhaps did not previously. In fact, it will result in the implementation of citizenship being about far more than the descriptors outlined in the National Curriculum, but will become about learning styles and the education of the whole child. In other words it will develop into something that frames a much larger picture than initially conceived. It will be organic in its evolution and impact, if and only if the leaders in the process do not become overly obsessed with the measurement of the quantifiable and tangible aspects of the Citizenship Order.

This is possibly a good time to raise the question of accountability! Accountable to whom? There can be and should only be one answer to this question: primarily, the student. There are inevitably other stakeholders interested in the process and outcomes of citizenship education, such as parents, employers, government and the wider community, but if we keep the child at the centre of our thinking then questions of accountability become less of a minefield and problematic. We are able to remind ourselves that the systems of accountability that we put in place are about helping students with their citizenship learning. Our procedures for assessment are about exactly that: giving feedback to learners about the progress they are making, so that future work can be aimed at further improvement.

An assessment-led curriculum, therefore, means that when planning programmes of study and schemes of work, assessment is an integral part of that process. When preparing what it is that students need to know, teachers are also planning how to assess and give feedback to students about what they have grasped and still need to revisit and learn. Likewise, the means by which children might assess themselves and each other or be assessed should be integrated into the planning about *how* they might learn the given subject or topic. Thus, what an assessment-driven curriculum should not be is a learning process dominated by a terminal summative assessment, otherwise known as accreditation!

Assessment and accreditation are not the same thing. Many appear to use the two terms in a synonymous way. Assessment is only really worthwhile if it is formative. It should be perceived as a different process from examining or testing when the only feedback tends to be an abstract signifier of attainment. If assessment is used as part of the ongoing dialogue between teacher and learner then there should be no concern about its function and role within citizenship education. Thus a school, when planning and implementing its citizenship curriculum should decide on a system for assessment that is appropriate to the way it teaches the subject.

The message is clear from government that schools should decide for themselves what is the most appropriate way to organise citizenship education to fulfil the requirements of the statutory orders. Our argument is that the message is equally applicable to assessment methods. Having made decisions about the purposes of their citizenship education programmes, schools should devise assessment schemes that relate to those purposes. How else can students and the other stakeholders know whether what was intended has been successfully achieved? This is where the wider elements of accountability come into play. Quite rightly, if a school has deployed resources and time into developing citizenship teaching, a means is required by which to measure how beneficial it has been. If the measurement process is directly connected to the learning objectives agreed at the time of planning the curriculum, then the accountability is an intrinsic mechanism, measuring what is valued. This avoids the danger of working only to criteria that are set externally, that are not sensitive to local situations and may lead to a perception that only the things that are measured are the things that are valued.

Moderation is a useful process and could even constitute a form of assessment. It would be a valid process to bring together exemplars of students' work and to evaluate how worthy the work is in terms of achieving the objectives of your citizenship education programme. Teachers are experienced at moderating coursework and discussing standards of students' attainment. Such a process could be applied for the assessment of the outcomes of a citizenship-focused scheme of work. The difference from the usual moderation process would be that the work is not pre-assessed. Instead, the students' work is presented for discussion about whether it fulfils the requirements of the citizenship programme of study. Does it meet expectation? Does it achieve what was intended?

An approach to assessment that starts with what the students' produce, rather than with abstract criteria, is more organic. It can then evolve a criterion that is based in practice and values that matter to the stakeholders, rather than skewing the teaching, learning and assessment towards what was initially thought to be measurable. It is a process that prefers to celebrate evidence of 'good' citizenship, rather than shaping the promotion of citizenship within a mould that has been defined in isolation of the 'citizens' whom it was intended to benefit. Surely, by definition, the development of citizenship has to be a person-centred activity.

Schools should identify within specific subject schemes of work, assignments that will demonstrate evidence of citizenship learning. A collation of those assignments would result in a Citizenship Portfolio, or 'progress file', and these would be used for the basis of the moderation/assessment process just outlined. Subject teachers would have marked the individual assignments in terms of the subject-specific criteria, and they could also have annotated the students' work with reference to its applicability to the citizenship objectives. The sum of those annotations alongside the evidence of the student's actual work would give sufficient material on which to make an assessment of the extent to which the intention and requirements of the citizenship education programme had been met. It is our contention that in many cases the dual approach to the teaching, learning and assessment of assignments will not only raise the level of citizenship awareness, it will also improve standards in the 'host' subject.

The other main advantage of the moderation approach to assessment is the staff development opportunities inherent within the process. Teachers looking together at students' work will then tend to discuss standards of achievement and variations in pedagogy that lead to examples of good practice. Teachers, possibly, will feel more willing and able to reflect constructively on their own teaching, lesson materials and motivational strategies in the relative security of a moderation meeting than in, say, a more formal appraisal situation. The further development that will occur in such a moderation context will be more organic and relative to the needs of the school community – staff and students alike.

Evolving criteria in the organic way described will lead on *naturally* to discussions about whether some exemplars of students' work display higher levels of citizenship competence than others. Questions will then emerge about the definition of 'citizenship

competence'. Is it to know more? Is it to be more factually accurate? Is it to be more inter-personally skilled? Is it to have a higher EQ (quota of emotional intelligence)? Is it to demonstrate considerable powers of empathy, persuasion and/or presence? The evolution of a quantitative element within a qualitative process may well lead to confusion about the purpose of the assessment. The issue may arise about whether assessment's primary function is formative and informs the teacher-learner dialogue, or is about differentiating whether one student is better at something than another. Or is the latter the purpose of accreditation? Or is the reason we differentiate attainment levels to recognise differences in achievement?

Whatever system of assessment is developed in a school, it must be linked to a process of recording. This is simply a professional responsibility, in case of the unforeseen and for reasons of continuity. Where assessment records are not kept, teachers ignore a sense of accountability to any one other than themselves. They cannot argue accountability still exists in the quality of their relationships with students, because what would happen if they were to 'fall under a bus'? The succeeding teacher would have no information and there would be the potential for the empty barrel syndrome. The other argument such a teacher might give would be that any records they kept would only mean something to themselves, and they would not be prepared to adopt more consensual signifiers for their own records because such abstractions would have too little meaning for them. Such arguments were abounded at the time when the 'secret classroom' of teacher autonomy was being challenged. The debate has moved on now and the pendulum cannot swing back from the acceptance that some form of common framework for curriculum and assessment is necessary to ensure proper coherence and continuity for students progressing through schooling. In addition, if the assessment approach is organic and evolutionary, as the moderation procedure implies, then teachers should feel reassured that the indicators representing achievement and attainment are well meant, have relevance and are specific in their meaning.

Most schools will have a policy with the title Assessment, Recording and Reporting. As argued above, assessments should be recorded. And records should be reported. Reported to whom? First and foremost to students, and then to other teachers who may have an interest or reason for knowing how a student has got on. Records also offer managers in school (and inspectors or advisors if required!) a means by which to carry out their monitoring and evaluation role. However, a main function of reporting is the accountability to parents. If students have undertaken a programme of citizenship education, and assessment and record keeping has been a logical part of that learning process, then a further consequence ought to be a report to parents outlining the progress that has been made. The report home is an affirmation of what the school values about citizenship education and communicates a summary of the information represented by the assessment and recording procedure. A school that has developed an approach to the assessment of citizenship, centred upon the outcomes achieved by students in relation to curriculum intentions will have little difficulty knowing how to report to parents on what their child has achieved. Likewise, recording systems that have been created that reflect succinctly the aims of the assessment foci will dovetail into a reporting format, which will also represent the purpose and essence of the citizenship programmes of study.

Reporting to student and parent is then a process by which to recognise achievement and acknowledge that which has been attained, instead of being a standalone activity that is not interconnected with the assessment and recording process. It is important that time is spent in getting right the interrelationship between assessment, recording and reporting, to ensure that the message that goes home is rooted in the learning objectives intended when deciding and devising the school's implementation of the Citizenship Order.

Assessment is not accreditation

It is probably possible to assess how well someone's citizenship skills, knowledge and attributes are progressing. It is less feasible to accredit it. When accrediting citizenship, what is being signified?

- The person is an accredited citizen?
- Certain skills have been acquired and even mastered?
- Knowledge regarding citizenship has been tested and enough was known to make the grade?
- A series of competencies have been assessed and these culminate in a certificate of achievement?
- A course of instruction/learning has been successfully completed?

Does the accreditation signal that the person receiving the 'certificate' will probably be a better citizen? Or that those not gaining the accreditation are 'failed' citizens?

What is important to establish is that assessment does not have to lead on to accreditation. They are separate things. Interestingly, the DfEE Working Group on Citizenship changed its terminology from 'accreditation' to 'recognising achievement'. This is probably in recognition of the issues outlined in the bullet points above. It is an encouraging sign that there is awareness at the 'centre' of the difficulties in how to verify externally a young person's learning and development in a subject like citizenship. Indeed, those working at the QCA have spoken about how assessment in citizenship needs to be different from more conventional forms in order to reflect the different nature of the subject. Time will tell whether politically this can happen, because there appears to be a fear that any precedent set with citizenship assessment and accreditation will influence changes in the accrediting of other subjects. What a real opportunity that would be!

As assessment is not accreditation, then schools do not have to accredit. It is a statutory requirement to have an end of Key Stage 3 assessment, but not so at Key Stage 4. An 'end of key stage description' exists for each key stage, and this is, so far, what the attainment target for each key stage consists of. It sets out 'the knowledge, skills and understanding that pupils of differing abilities and maturates are expected to have by the end of a key stage'. The quotation is the definition given by the Education Act 1996, section 353a.

The National Curriculum Order for citizenship states the following, under the heading 'Assessing attainment at the end of a key stage': 'As citizenship will not be introduced until 2002, further information about assessment will be available in due course'. Although it is understandable that schools might do nothing about the assessment of citizenship because of the above statement, it is not wise, because of the arguments outlined earlier. A school must have addressed questions relating to assessment if teachers, students and parents are to value the implementation of citizenship education. They should not, for all the reasons given previously, plan their approach for the teaching of citizenship without also deciding upon their methodology for assessment, recording and reporting. A school that does this will have the courage of their convictions to continue with what they believe is most appropriate for their community when in due course further information becomes available. If that new information suggests an approach different from that which the school has planned, then the school can decide which is better – the QCA one or their own. We should always accept changing something if we can see that the alternative is a superior model. And the reason for working on your own solution until the government's arrives is because theirs, if superior, will be more acceptable on account of there being the comparison. Having established your preferred practice, if the newer model is better it will be evident that this is so, and will be therefore more palatable than if there were no benchmark.

In contrast, if what is presented is not as good as what the school has evolved, then the external framework should be 're-presented' and interpreted so that the superior internal model is able to accommodate it! It should not be too difficult to address external requirements if the in-house approach is of high quality. In this way the school can 'protect' what it believes is the most worthwhile system for its students. This may be of particular importance if the reference to 'levels' in the National Curriculum Citizenship Order becomes anything more than a reference to the fact that other subjects have levels of attainment.

'The expectation at the end of key stage 3 matches the level of demand in other subjects and is broadly equivalent to levels 5/6' (National Curriculum Citizenship Key Stages 3–4; DfEE/QCA 1999). Does this quotation imply the possibility of attaining a level 3 or 4 at Key Stage 3, or a level 6 or above at Key Stage 4? We would argue that the application of levels of attainment in citizenship is an ill-advised route. As pointed out earlier, it may become inevitable that schools wish to differentiate between achievements in citizenship education, but will they want an overarching standard of attainment? What is more likely is that teachers will wish to recognise differences in achievement in a particular aspect of the citizenship programmes of study. Hence, the portfolio approach to assessment, and an accreditation system that accredits things as they are achieved, would be more appropriate. An accumulative framework which is not tied to the end of a key stage, but that allows a young person to accredit things as they achieve them, will have the flexibility to remain relevant to students as they each develop in their individual way. Awards already exist, such as ASDAN and the Duke of Edinburgh Award scheme, which have such a framework. It is difficult to see how a GCSE in citizenship will have the necessary flexibility.

Schools would be advised to think very carefully before subscribing to formal accreditation at the end of Key Stage 4. The pressure to offer an exam because otherwise students will not consider citizenship a worthwhile subject, and/or the school wants the higher grades it might produce, should be resisted. The implementation of a citizenship education programme should be for its intrinsic purposes and worth. The introduction of an examination may cause the teaching of the subject to become more about gaining the accreditation than about the development of the citizen.

Schools may be advised to watch carefully the development of the following:

- key skills and their accreditation;
- those key skills not presently accredited;
- citizenship education Post 16 and the influence of the Learning Skills Councils;
- literacy, numeracy and ICT from Key Stage 3 into 4 (recent consultation on target setting at Key Stage 3 included ICT);
- the impact of dis-application from subjects at Key Stage 4;
- increasing localised control of schools; and
- teacher shortages and performance management.

The contention is that all of these could have an effect on the impact of citizenship education in schools. It would be beyond the remit of this chapter to discuss these at greater length, except to say that they provide all the more reason that schools must be true to themselves and ensure that their approach to the Citizenship Order and its implementation is done in such a way as to enhance and further promote the values and aims of their organisation. In conclusion, I would say that schools must start with the good practice that already exists in and out of their classrooms. Where there are gaps, worry about those later, and plug them into your evolved concept/framework once it is truly and securely in place

CHAPTER 4

Curriculum projects in citizenship

A curriculum which acknowledges the social responsibilities of education must present situations where problems are relevant to the problems of living together, and where observation and information are calculated to develop social insight and interests.

(John Dewey 1926: 226)

Introduction

The above quotation by John Dewey gives emphasis to *relevancy* as a prime principle for curriculum design. The same principle motivates the work of the Coalition for Citizenship which is comprised of organisations that seek, in large part, to develop and support relevant education for an active citizenship. These organisations promote citizenship education in schools by means of:

a) advice on and production of a range of citizenship resources;
b) provision of teaching materials, packages and programmes for citizenship;
c) citizenship award schemes for schools;
d) research in citizenship teaching in schools;
e) school curriculum projects in citizenship;
f) community involvement programmes;
g) staff development materials and INSET; and
h) qualifications in citizenship.

These are private organisations and therefore their resources and capacity to support and cover effectively all the schools in England is limited. However, they have had a major influence on the promotion of citizenship education and have also been innovative in terms of curriculum projects in schools. This chapter will detail these organisations and provide some illustrative examples of how they have developed curriculum programmes for schools. This chapter will also look at how the DfEE has established a Working Party for Citizenship Education which is charged with providing detailed guidance for schools in 2001 on implementing citizenship education. Advice in the following areas will be offered to schools: teacher training, assessment, community involvement and sharing good practice and resources.

Objectives

At the end of this chapter you will have been introduced to:

- the work of a number of citizenship organisations in education;
- examples of school-based curriculum projects in citizenship education; and
- the themes developed for guidance by the Working Party For Citizenship Education.

Organisations supporting education for citizenship

The following provides a description of the organisations that make up the Coalition for Citizenship and provides, by way of illustration, examples of the kinds of school-based curriculum projects, evaluations and programmes they are currently sponsoring. The DfEE are also funding these organisations to produce resources for schools and to provide conferences for potential teachers of citizenship education.

The Centre for Citizenship Studies in Education

School of Education, University of Leicester, 21 University Road, Leicester LE1 7RF
Tel: **0116 2523681**   Fax: **0116 2523653**   e-mail: **ccse@le.ac.uk**
Internet: **http://www.le.ac.uk/education/centres/citizenship/cs.html**

The centre for Citizenship Studies in Education (CCSE) exists to promote training, research and consultancy for citizenship, human rights and the teaching of democracy in schools. It aims to develop and disseminate good practice in this field. Since it was set up in 1991 it has played a prominent part in developments at national and international levels, with staff working closely with organisations such as the Council of Europe, the European Commission and Amnesty International. The Centre offers an accredited distance learning course *Learning for Citizenship* in the UK and internationally. CCSE specialises in issues of race, ethnicity and diversity in education.

Some activities of the Centre

1. Economic and Social Research Council seminar series:
   Human Rights and Democracy in Schools 1998–2000.
2. Membership of Economic and Social Research Council committee for research initiative on Youth Society and Citizenship.
3. Research on behalf of the DfEE into reasons for exclusion from school 1999.
4. European Commission thematic network on Intercultural Education and Global Citizenship 1999–2001.
5. Providing rapporteur to the series of Council of Europe/University of Uppsala annual conferences on the Teaching of Democratic Citizenship.
6. Consultancy for the Department for International Development on development education 1999–2000.
7. Consultant to several NFER projects including the International Evaluation of Education Achievement (Civics).
8. Founder member of the Values Education Council of UK.
9. Founder member of the Coalition for Citizenship which is a collaborative network of organisations supporting education for citizenship.
10. Member of steering group for the Oxford, Cambridge and RSA examinations (OCR) Citizenship Awards Steering Committee.
11. Member of Citizenship Consultation Group convened by Professor Bernard Crick following the publication of *Education for Citizenship and the Teaching of Democracy in Schools* (Crick Report).
12. Termly mailing of newsletter and enclosures to 1,500 recipients without charge to them – these include teachers, teacher educators, opinion formers, advisors and inspectors, LEA officers, youth workers, voluntary organisations…
13. Evaluation of a curriculum development project in Northern Ireland run by the Citizenship Foundation and the University of Ulster.

The Citizenship Foundation

Ferroness House, Shaftesbury Place, Off Aldersgate Street, London EC2Y 8AA
Tel: **020 7367 0500**   Fax: **020 7367 0501**   e-mail: **info@citfou.org.uk**
Internet: **http://www.citfou.org.uk**

The Citizenship Foundation was established in 1989, to promote better quality citizenship education in schools and the wider community, through curriculum development, teacher training and support, public information and adult education and through the provision of active learning experiences for young people. It also undertakes relevant research. Its mission statement links individuals' right to know about their rights and responsibilities with society's need for a well-informed citizenry, committed to values of democracy and human rights. The foundation's earliest curriculum work was through the national Law in Education Project, run in cooperation with the National Curriculum Council. This was the first National Curriculum development to address the issue of teaching all young people *as an entitlement* about their rights and responsibilities as citizens and the role of law in society. This work foreshadowed and helped to inform the introduction in 1989 of citizenship as a cross-curricular theme of the new National Curriculum.

The core work of the foundation has been curriculum development and teacher training. By 1992, law-related material had been produced for both Key Stages 3 and 4[1] and this was followed by work aimed at primary students. Continuity and progression through key stages was achieved by the development of a single framework of *core concepts*, including rights, duties, justice, power, rules, laws, diversity and so on. Primary pupils are introduced to these ideas through the use of narrative[2], and an analytical methodology in which the teacher facilitates a shared deconstruction of the text in terms of the social and moral issues raised. This is intended both to deepen children's understanding of ideas which are central to moral and political discourse (which are already under development during the primary years) and also to nurture the skills of critical thinking and debate as well as promoting attitudes of respect for diversity and democracy.

In 1996, the Citizenship Foundation undertook further development work aimed at the secondary curriculum. The Moral Education in Secondary Schools Project[3] set out to provide materials which would assist students throughout the secondary years (Y7–Y13) to understand those forms of moral thought and argument which are present in public moral discourse. The materials aim to equip students to engage with others, to argue a point of view or simply to think about citizenship issues with greater clarity and awareness. This concept-based approach has broken new ground in moving moral education beyond the rehearsal of 'big issues' such as abortion or the over-narrow discussion of Kohlbergian moral dilemmas. In September 2000, a new project was embarked on which is attempting to do the same for those major political ideas which inform political thought. This is to move beyond the more established definition of 'political literacy' as the transmission of useful knowledge of the political system and the encouragement of a proclivity to become actively involved in the political realm.

The Citizenship Foundation's curriculum development work is characterised by the attempt to integrate fully the development of conceptual understanding and the skills of analysis and debate with the acquisition of essential social and political knowledge. The citizen is seen as a moral agent, and while young citizens need to be aware of their rights and responsibilities, it is also essential that they develop morally in the Kohlbergian sense of progressing from the immature, egocentric concerns towards becoming more sociocentric and sensitive in their outlook.

The Crick Report on the teaching of citizenship and democracy in schools which led to the introduction of the statutory orders for citizenship in 2000, endorsed this concept-based approach, in emphasising that the development of social and moral responsibility was as important an element of citizenship teaching as political literacy.

Teacher training, both nationally and internationally, has always been an important element of the Citizenship Foundation's work with a significant number of overseas training and development projects being undertaken, notably in the countries of the former Soviet Union. At home, the foundation has recently embarked on a new type of teacher training project with the development of a 'distance learning' package for primary schools, called 'Introducing Citizenship'[4]. The centrepiece of the pack is a video with three extended sequences showing teachers at work with children, discussing a range of citizenship issues. The video is to be used by teachers for critical analysis in training situations. The accompanying trainer's handbook suggests how these sequences can be used to focus on different elements of the teaching situation, including evaluating the effectiveness of different teaching techniques and relating children's responses to what is known about the psychology of child development. The handbook also provides considerable background information on many other aspects of education for citizenship including a range of whole-school issues such as the value of establishing a school council. This is the subject of the final section of the video programme.

In addition to these facets of its work, the foundation undertakes research, two significant pieces of work being into democracy in schools and into the nature of citizenship-promoting activities in the informal youth sector. The foundation also runs seminars, events and competitions for schools, to provide some hands-on experience of the legal and parliamentary systems. The most notable of these are the Mock Trial Competitions using real magistrates, barristers and judges in Magistrates courts (for lower secondary pupils) and in Crown Courts (for senior secondary pupils). The Youth Parliament Competition (sponsored by Motorola) invites students to simulate a parliamentary-style debate on a topic of their choice, the winning teams coming together for live debates and visits to the House of Commons to meet senior politicians.

Notes

1. *Living with the Law* and *Understand the Law* for Key Stages 3 and 4 respectively, by Don Rowe and Tony Thorpe. Published by Hodder and Stoughton.
2. *You, Me, Us!* By Don Rowe and Jan Newton, published by the Home Office, 1994.
3. Published as *Good Thinking, books 1–3,* by Evans Bros., 2000. Written by Ted Huddleston and Don Rowe.
4. *Introducing Citizenship* by Don Rowe is published by A & C Black, 2001, as a handbook with video, accompanied by four exemplar stories for Key Stage 1.

Institute for Citizenship

62 Marylebone High Street, London W1U 5HZ
Tel: **020 7935 4777**   Fax: **020 7486 9212**   e-mail: **info@citizen.org.uk**
Internet: **http://www.citizen.org.uk**

The Institute for Citizenship was established in 1992 and aims to promote informed, active citizenship and greater participation in democracy and society. It attempts to achieve this through the provision of innovative and stimulating projects and through working with schools to develop materials which meet the requirements of citizenship education as a new National Curriculum subject.

Curriculum Project: Citizenship at Key Stage 3

Over two years the Institute (in partnership with schools in Halton, Leicester, Derby, Tower Hamlets, Hackney and Islington) will develop exemplars of effective practice across the key stage and across the ability range.

Inclusion is at the heart of the work undertaken. A number of schools for children with severe and multiple learning difficulties are involved in the project, working closely with Adam Newman Turner (Associate Manager for Inclusion in Citizenship) and building links with mainstream local schools as well as other special schools.

The outcome of this project will contribute to the development of all students at Key Stage 3, recognising their diverse abilities and needs, as well as to the development of the school both as a community in its own right and as a cornerstone of the local community which it serves.

The educational resources developed through the project will deliver the content element of the curriculum so that students better understand their rights, responsibilities and the world in which they exercise them. The institute will also be working closely with teachers and other professionals throughout the project to develop models of successful practice which help students build their skills of participation and reflection to enable them to become effective active citizens.

The Institute is also running a project for Key Stage 4 pupils and producing a series of textbooks and accessible materials for citizenship lessons.

CSV Education for Citizenship

237 Pentonville Road, London N1 9NJ
Tel: **020 7278 6601**   Fax: **020 7713 0560**   e-mail: **education@csv.org.uk**
Internet: **http://www.csv.org.uk/CSV/Education/education.htm**

Community Service Volunteers (CSV) was established in 1962 to promote away-from-home volunteering in the UK. Community Service Volunteers have since developed a range of additional activities to foster volunteering and community participation in education, training and public service of all kinds. Community Service Volunteers' Education for Citizenship, a division of CSV, works with schools, colleges and universities to involve young people in citizenship education through active learning in the community. Citizenship education links learning with action and action with learning in and beyond the classroom; it helps young people become articulate, active and responsible members of their communities.

Higher education

In higher education CSV has launched the Council for Citizenship and Learning in the Community (CCLC). The council has grown from the network of universities with whom we have been associated over the past 10 years. The CCLC also provides a strong platform on which to bring together and further strengthen CSV's range of initiatives in higher education, including student tutoring and community partnerships.

In the past year *CSV Learning Together,* our student tutoring programme, has continued to offer university students as tutors in secondary, primary and special schools. Each year around 7,000 students from 160 universities and colleges throughout the UK volunteer in local schools, helping pupils with their studies, acting as positive role models and encouraging young people to continue on to further or higher education.

We have supported the government's literacy campaign and the National Year of Reading (NYR) through our paired reading programme, *CSV Reading Together.*

Working with schools

Our work with schools has also developed strongly over the past year. The *Barclays New Futures* award scheme, the *CSV Lighthouse Schools* and *CSV Discovering Citizenship* have each continued to play a crucial part in the development of citizenship education through active learning in the community.

Barclays New Futures

This major programme – the biggest single sponsorship for schools – supports community initiatives in some 300 schools each year. The awards of cash, materials and advice are made to secondary schools that come up with the best ideas for social action projects linked with real learning. Community Service Volunteers provides professional support, monitoring and advice through our team of advisers. We work closely with the sponsorship agency to promote the programme nation-wide and meet regularly with Barclays Bank.

Barclays New Futures now publishes a series of brief guides to assist teachers in implementing citizenship projects. The initial booklet is a simple introduction to the scheme illustrated with text and pictures showing how active learning in the community develops vital skills for life, work and citizenship.

During the course of the year we have on several occasions used Barclays New Futures case studies in evidence to government departments and agencies. We plan to publish a collection of these case studies to stimulate and encourage teachers with ideas and suggestions drawn from real-life projects.

CSV Lighthouse Schools

We are continuing to work with our Lighthouse Schools and their associates to provide evidence of the most effective ways in which senior managers can introduce citizenship education across the life of the whole school. The project concentrates on curriculum, staff development and teacher training. We shall distil what we have learnt in a publication aimed at heads, senior managers and governors.

In addition to our work with the Roehampton Institute on initial teacher training and professional development, we are developing work in Birmingham on the link between citizenship education and PSHE.

CSV Discovering Citizenship

Community Service Volunteers Discovering Citizenship provides classroom teachers with a tried and tested programme of work for secondary pupils. It was initially pioneered by our colleagues in the United States and has now been developed in an English context. During the past year the Deutsche Bank has sponsored us to develop and disseminate training and materials in 22 London secondary schools. Bank staff have also volunteered their time as mentors and tutors in the schools, thus further enriching the programme. We have also developed a primary version during a highly successful demonstration project at Primrose Hill School in North London.

Healthy Schools Project

We have been proud to develop a partnership with Pennywell School in Sunderland on healthy living. This has involved volunteers supporting pupils in their peer mentoring initiatives to reduce bullying and to promote healthy living. In this we have enjoyed the support of the Department of Health.

Peer mentoring

We have continued to develop work on peer mentoring which we plan to make available later through our Training and Services Unit.

Regional and local partnerships

Where possible we set out to establish local and regional staff in partnership with local organisations. We are currently working with Barking and Rotherham.

Council for Education in World Citizenship

Sir John Lyon House, 5 High Timber Street, London EC4V 3PA
Tel: **020 7329 1500**   Fax: **020 7328 8160**   e-mail: **info@cewc.org.uk**
Internet: **URL://www.cewc.org.uk**

The Council for Education in World Citizenship offers pupils and teachers a range of active learning opportunities to help them understand the connections between the local, national and global dimensions of issues. These include Model United Nations events and workshops on sustainable development and corporate citizenship. Negotiated Learning is a project that involves pupils and teachers in the design of teaching and learning about citizenship. Beginning with an initial group of 14 young people aged 11 to 16 we generated a questionnaire in four sections. The first section gives a list of 'burning issues', the second styles of teaching, the third learning methods and the fourth looks at school councils. Over 300 young people completed the pilot questionnaire. They were asked to rank statements in each section according to the level of importance they attached to it. They were also asked to indicate any words or phrases whose meaning was not clear to them. There was space to add their own comments. The questionnaire serves a dual purpose. It provides young people with different aspects of education for global citizenship. This can inform both teachers and resource providers. At the same time it can be used to provide a stimulus for discussion. Negotiated Learning is part of a process of teaching young people as citizens, engaging them with their learning more as partners than recipients. The 'burning issues' which pupils felt should form the content of citizenship education are as follows (Table 4.1) , in order of preference.

Table 4.1

Issue/Topic	Average Score (out of 5)
Racism/minorities/gender	4.4
Pollution throughout the world	4.2
Child labour – fair wages and conditions of work	4.1
Universality of rights – everyone equally entitled?	4.0
Human rights within and between generations	4.0
Destruction of the rain forests	4.0
Teenagers' rights to make decisions for themselves	3.9
Recycling	3.9
Endangered species – particularly the panda, tiger, white rhino	3.9
Poverty	3.8
Genetically modified (GM) foods	3.8
Humanitarian aid	3.8
Fair Trade and the Third World	3.8
Religion/culture	3.8
Diversity of national, regional, religious and ethnic identities	3.7
Media and freedom of expression	3.5
Globalisation, economics and inequality	3.5
Refugees' rights	3.4
Political system-democracy	3.3
Sustainable development	3.3
Power of richer companies	3.1
Advertising directed at young people	3.1

The full report may be obtained from Gabby Rowberry at the address above.

The Hansard Society

St. Philips Building North, Sheffield Street, London WC2A 2EX
Tel: **020 7955 7478** Fax: **020 7955 7492**   e-mail: **hansard@hansard.lse.ac.uk**
Internet: **http://www.hansardsociety.org.uk**

The Hansard Society promotes effective parliamentary democracy and aims to assist the process of modernising the parliamentary system. It is concerned with promoting experiential learning in democratic education in schools. Its website contains an excellent interactive introduction to the workings of Parliament.

In addition to the above organisations which have formed a coalition, there are at least three other organisations which are worth mentioning. First, Schools Council UK is an organisation that has been working for the last 10 years to help train teachers and pupils to establish democratic structures in schools so as to increase pupil involvement. It does this through advice and training on how to establish school councils, class councils and a peer-developed charter of behaviour and peer management. Second, the Council for Environmental Education provides schools with information on sustainable development – particularly a list of all the organisations associated with sustainable development and the kinds of resources they provide for schools. Third, The British Council provides information on most countries around the world. The coalition has also founded the Association of Citizenship Teachers together with a professional journal entitled *Teaching Citizenship*. These developments help mark citizenship education as a main subject on the school curriculum.

As indicated earlier these organisations are being funded by the DfEE to produce resources as part of a package of support to develop citizenship education in schools. In 2001 the DfEE provided £550,000 to develop the following projects alone: Young People's Passport (Citizenship Foundation); Election Pack website (Institute for Citizenship); Toolkit for School Councils (SCUK); Mock Elections Y Vote (Hansard); and a Directory of Community Organisations (CSV). In the same year the government has provided £12,000,000 for schools as part of the Standards Fund to support the delivery of citizenship education and will provide a further £15,000,000 in 2002. The DfEE Working Party for Citizenship Education advises ministers on the implementation of citizenship.

Working Party for citizenship education

This DfEE Working Party was established to support the implementation of the Citizenship Order and is currently considering what guidance should be offered to schools. The working party had established four sub-groupings to address the following areas:

1. Teacher training.
2. Assessment.
3. Community involvement.
4. Sharing good practice and resources.

However, before the sub-groups met, the DfEE and Teacher Training Agency had decided to proceed with making available to higher education institutions a small number of citizenship education specialist places as part of the initial teacher training targets in secondary subjects for 2001. Citizenship has also been added to the priority areas for continuing professional development and every secondary school was allocated a sum of money in April 2000 to assist with the preparations in implementing citizenship education. The initial teacher training targets for history and geography were initially increased to cater for the extra demand for teachers who could teach citizenship. There is also the possibility of setting up summer schools for teachers to develop their subject knowledge in citizenship education. The sub-groups identified a number of training needs for teachers including: subject knowledge, pedagogy, organisation and curriculum issues and community involvement. A training needs analysis was produced for the implementation of citizenship education.

There was discussion of how teachers might be trained to manage active learning in schools and in the community especially given that there was less of a traditional teaching role and more of a coordinating role in working in partnership with others in and outside of the school. How teachers are trained in assessing community involvement and how to involve pupils in deciding on, planning, carrying out and evaluating community involvement activities was also discussed. In the assessment sub-group it was recognised that assessing citizenship education was not new since examination boards and other organisations were already developing qualifications. It was also identified that Key Stage 4 is a difficult area for assessment, but that short GCSE courses and perhaps key skill awards with pupils compiling portfolios of evidence of citizenship learning were good ways forward. It was felt that assessment should be rigorous if it was to carry weight and credibility, but that any guidelines for schools should adopt a light-touch approach.

The Minister for Schools, Jackie Smith, wrote to all members of these sub-groups in the summer of 2000 to thank them for their work to date, but informing them that the main working party had decided to proceed without sub-groups. However, the teacher training sub-group continued to meet at the Teacher Training Agency and commissioned research to establish whether or not there was a demand in secondary schools for NQ citizenship teachers. A representative sample of 237 schools responded to telephone interviews and 80 per cent of these interviews were conducted with headteachers in the sample – the other 20 per cent with senior staff responsible for the curriculum. Many of the respondents, especially in the large cities, confirmed that they would employ a specialist citizenship teacher, but the overwhelming majority did expect such a teacher to teach a second subject. This second subject, in order of preference by the schools that responded, was PSHE, history, social studies and religious education. Meanwhile the Teacher Training Agency invited teacher educators to bid for citizenship numbers, either as a specialist subject or as a combined subject. The vast majority of teacher educators in higher education bid for these places which is interesting considering that research by UNICEF (2000: 4) found that most initial and postgraduate teacher educators considered that they had insufficient time to prepare students for citizenship education.

The DfEE is concerned to identify 'good practice' in citizenship education on the ground in schools. To this end it and the QCA are looking at what is going on in Educational Action Zones, Beacon Schools, Excellence in Cities and the Coalition for Citizenship Education curriculum projects and resources. The DfEE have funded and sponsored a number of curriculum projects with these organisations together with launching its own citizenship website in summer 2001. This site is intended to provide a gateway to key information on citizenship education and to support teacher needs with examples of good practice. The DfEE has also established a group on Teacher Training and

Continuing Professional Development in the area of citizenship education to advise it on policy. The department has also undertaken research through the NFER to survey what is being done in other countries.

The Qualifications and Curriculum Authority (QCA) is also involved in providing information about curriculum and qualification developments in citizenship education in partnership with the DfEE. In particular, the QCA has established a group, comprised mainly of teachers, to provide schools with schemes of work for citizenship education at Key Stages 1 to 4. The intention at secondary level is threefold: to show how teachers can make use of the flexibility available within the programmes of study for citizenship; to make links to other National Curriculum subjects; and to provide examples of appropriate means of assessment. The QCA seeks to provide local education authority advisors and advisory teachers with advance notification about its own forthcoming publications and to disseminate information about developments in citizenship education more widely in the teaching profession. It also provides guidance, such as 'Developing a global dimension in the school curriculum', which shows how a global dimension can be incorporated into both the curriculum and the wider life of the school. However, perhaps the most important development for citizenship teachers will be the schemes of work which will be published during 2001. These schemes are not written like other National Curriculum subject schemes, but are more flexible and can be used in a variety of ways by teachers. Ruth Tudor addresses these issues in more detail in chapter eight.

There are separate schemes of work for both Key Stages 3 and 4 and each contains a teacher's guide together with units that provide possible teaching activities, learning outcomes and opportunities for assessment. The schemes of work also link to other National Curriculum subjects and to PSHE and show ways of making citizenship education more explicit in the wider curriculum, the whole school and out of school. Indeed, they were written with existing subjects in mind so that citizenship lessons could use much of the materials in existing school subjects. Emphasis is also given to examples of activities that enable pupils to contribute to and participate in the life of their school and their communities. These schemes of work are available on the DfEE Standards website (http://www.standards.dfee.giov.uk).

At post-16, it was recognised that because of the diverse and varied menu of subjects taken by students it would be difficult to incorporate citizenship education into a voluntary curriculum. However, the Advisory Group for Citizenship 16–19 Year Olds, chaired by Professor Bernard Crick, reported that 16–19 year olds should have some entitlement to citizenship education (the report can be found at http://www.fefc.ac.uk). The report recommends that skills for active citizenship should form part of the post-16 curriculum and should build on pre-16 courses. These skills are identified as research, advocacy, conciliation, leadership, representation and evaluation. Values, such as promoting the common good, are also recognised as having an important place in further education. The government has given responsibility for developing these recommendations, particularly that young adults should develop and apply citizenship-specific skills to the Learning and

Skills Development Agency which has invited post-16 educational institutions to bid for funds to develop curriculum projects for the 16–19 curriculum. These curriculum projects are expected to be available in 2002. It can be seen that there are a variety of curriculum projects in citizenship education being initiated by government, government agencies, but particularly by private bodies interested in promoting citizenship education in schools.

Tasks

TASK 4.1

Compare and contrast two of the private organisations mentioned above that have devised curriculum projects in citizenship. In what ways do their conceptions of 'citizenship' differ?

TASK 4.2

Consult the Crick Report. Compare this with the citizenship order. In what way do they support, add or differ from each other? What conception of citizenship is presented in the Crick Report?

CHAPTER 5

Teaching and learning in citizenship

When dealing with controversial issues, teachers should adopt strategies that teach pupils how to recognise bias, how to evaluate evidence put before them and how to look for alternative interpretations, viewpoints and sources of evidence, above all to give good reasons for everything they say and do, and to expect good reasons to be given by others.

(QCA: 1998: 65)

Introduction

Teachers are familiar with the aims of their subject, its content and the different strategies that can be used to teach it in order to bring about the desired learning in the pupil. They will also be aware of the fact that there are many different ways to learn their subject and that the process of learning can be both intentional and unintentional. Indeed, they will also recognise that human beings have a natural capacity to learn and that they learn an impressive amount prior to arriving in school. Many teachers will also recognise that the study of citizenship is essentially the study of human activity in its moral, social and political forms and that consequently these human dimensions are often controversial since they cannot always be settled by appeals to facts or evidence and are therefore contested. This is often used to argue that such study should be excluded from the school curriculum. Teachers who have taught personal and social education will also realise that understanding of these dimensions of human activity is often based on the experiences of the pupil which includes their feelings, emotions and passions as well as their intellect. Pupils come to school already attached to different values. There is therefore an essential behavioural dimension to citizenship education which seeks to help pupils to prepare for adult life.

Citizenship education is about exploring from different perspectives what it means to be human. It is also about participation in or membership of a community. Teachers are the human point of contact with pupils and it is they who mediate many of the other influences on the learning of pupils. Ultimately, it is the teacher who will determine the quality of citizenship education offered in school. Teachers of citizenship education will invariably use many of the teaching strategies already well established in other subjects together with their skills of managing the learning experiences of pupils in the classroom. However, these strategies will need to emphasise the application of knowledge to many sensitive settings and contexts within human activity and teachers will also need to feel confident about their knowledge of citizenship and how it might be taught. A reading of the huge amount of literature on teaching and learning simply serves to convince teachers that no single teaching strategy would be satisfactory in citizenship. Citizenship education is about inculcating values and many believe that the teaching and learning of citizenship is therefore more important than the content because the teaching will express the real intentions of the teacher. Griffith (1998) argues strongly that the current National Curriculum and the structure of subjects within it lead to a factual transmission of knowledge which is not effective in the development of the attributes of citizenship. He emphasises 'socially placed learning' and seeks 'critically reflective, morally autonomous and socially active citizens'. He believes that citizenship education should be entirely child-centred and aim to develop citizens through the pupils' own exploration of their rights and responsibilities via personal action within the school (1998: 33). Griffith presents us with a radical approach to teaching and learning in citizenship which is worthy of considerable attention, but this chapter has a more limited aim which seeks to remind teachers of the kinds of strategies for teaching and learning which would be appropriate to citizenship education within the present school framework.

Objectives

At the end of this chapter you will have understood:

a) why teaching and learning in citizenship is controversial;
b) different strategies for teaching citizenship education;
c) the importance of the affective domain in teaching and learning citizenship education; and
d) an understanding of bias and critical thinking.

Theoretical background

If teachers are expected to be 'authorities' in their subject areas, in terms of their knowledge and application, then no less so should the teacher of citizenship be a 'subject authority'. This may mean that each school will need to provide some professional development for selected staff or appoint new staff with the knowledge and teaching skills necessary to deliver citizenship in the curriculum. In particular, it will require a fresh look at teaching and learning in the school, especially if there has been an emphasis on didactic teaching methods with pupils generally passive, viewing learning as preparation for examinations. If this situation persists then it will be a difficult school culture to change. The teacher also cannot be completely neutral in their teaching as there are frequent occasions when they must intervene – when pupils display overt sexism or racism they cannot go unchallenged by the teacher. Teachers cannot be indifferent to these important matters for if they remained impartial then they would cease to be positive educators. It is our view that teachers should be able to express their own views in the classroom, when appropriate, without advocating them. In any case, we know that the development of a pupil's capacity to reason about questions of moral conduct does not necessarily result in a change of conduct – one cannot reason one's way to virtuous citizenship.

However, use here could be made of the work Lawrence Stenhouse has undertaken in teaching controversial subjects. In his well-known work with the Humanities Curriculum Project he made popular the idea of the 'impartial chairperson' by which the teacher avoids stating his or her own position and keeps to procedural rules – in effect the teacher renounces their authority as 'expert'. Evidence is respected and the pupils' statements and viewpoints, however inaccurate, are deemed important. The idea behind this teaching method was the development of the autonomy of the child which meant the avoidance of any potential beliefs or morals in teaching. Basil Singh has written against this neutrality idea on the basis that whether it is evidence or argument it is someone's interpretation. Is it not also the case that some kinds of evidence are more relevant or more compelling than others and that teachers should be in a better position than their pupils to assess the various views and claims made upon evidence in relation to certain topics? Stenhouse (1981: 103–5) researched his own 'impartial chair' teaching method and found that attitudes and values were formed regardless of the method. Pupils were just as likely to be influenced at home and he reminded us that pupils are not *tabulae rasae*.

With a central government-sponsored Citizenship Order some believe that this could leave schools and their pupils open to political manipulation and indoctrination. Those who become citizenship teachers have not entered the teaching profession to propagandise on behalf of the state. Peter Kellner said of citizenship in the *Independent* in 1988: 'It is a precious, exhilarating, anti-establishment word which politicians the world over have tried to steal. Only in dictatorships and enfeebled democracies do they ever succeed'. Similarly there have also been some fears among teachers about indoctrination and authoritarian approaches that they believed have the potential to create an ethos of compliance in schools and encourage conformity and passivity in pupils. The question of neutrality and indoctrination has been discussed at length in the literature and this chapter will make passing reference to them. What is often more important is the personality and values of the teacher and how these are reflected in the life of the classroom. In a sense there is little that can be done about these personal qualities in the teacher. Another important point to understand is that some teachers of citizenship will favour a largely content-based approach, while others will favour an emphasis on teaching methods as the best way to teach citizenship education.

Davies (1994) has shown how political themes in the 1950s were taught as facts with a focus on information about democracy taught through information packs, textbooks and teacher talk – which were often removed from the everyday experience of the pupils. In the 1960s and 70s there was greater emphasis on skills to effect change while in the 1980s the experience and values of the pupil began to be considered. Today, parents might object to either the inclusion of certain topics in the curriculum or to the way a subject is taught. There is a need to identify specific areas of teaching and learning which are peculiar to citizenship education. We will look at just a few of the elements important in citizenship education and these areas are bias, critical thinking and controversial issues as central to teaching citizenship. In the next chapter we shall explore the meaning and application of experiential learning. All of these overlap with each other and need to be considered together.

Different strategies for teaching citizenship

Teaching the abstract

Perhaps the most immediate problem that teachers of citizenship face is that of how to teach abstract or complicated principles in an engaging and imaginative manner. Much of the proposed content of citizenship relates to these abstract and fundamental principles. Among these are included concepts such as rights and duties, power and authority, identities, representation and change and the way in which conflict can be resolved. How is the teacher to teach such profound concepts and, of equal and connected importance, how are pupils to learn them?

Before teachers can teach such concepts they must first be clear themselves about what they mean and what their implications are. The first point of reference, then, would be to attempt a definition of the terms, since these have been largely left out of the Order. In identifying and defining these principles pupils will be guarded against being presented with a seemingly random and unconnected pepperpot of examples. Such a superficial treatment runs the risk of becoming either completely descriptive or completely meaningless, or both, with the pupils unclear as to what it is they are actually studying and indeed why they are bothering to study it at all. Focusing in on dry and arid principles will not enable pupils to see the relevance they have to their lives, neither will such an approach enable pupils to achieve the end of moving from a cognitive style of learning to one which affects their behaviour for the better. With these fundamental principles of citizenship now clarified, two effective and connected strategies can be used to teach the abstract principles of citizenship: these are teaching by analogy and deducing fundamental principles from familiar contexts and surroundings.

Teaching by deductive reasoning

Once the principles of citizenship have been defined and clarified, think of relating them to situations or circumstances with which the pupils will be familiar. Deductive reasoning focuses on allowing pupils to analyse the surroundings to situations around them and from these to formulate general principles. A first point of access here could be to ask pupils to list what rights they have and what duties they think they have. They could then be asked to correspond the rights to the duties, as far as is possible. This could be done as individuals, in pairs, in groups or as a whole-class discussion. After such a general discussion, the lesson could then focus on identifying differing rights and duties within differing contexts. A lesson, or a sequence of lessons on rights and duties, for example, could use the following questions to guide responses and understanding:

1. What are our entitlements and obligations within the classroom?
2. What are our entitlements and obligations within the school?
3. What are our entitlements and obligations beyond the school gates?
4. What are our entitlements and obligations within the country as a whole?
5. What are our entitlements and obligations when we visit other countries?
6. What are the entitlements and obligations between countries?

Following such an approach should enable pupils to move from a recognition of the immediate examples surrounding them to a definition of the principles underlying such examples and an application of these definitions or principles to other contexts and situations.

Teaching by analogy

Closely connected to teaching by deductive reasoning is teaching by analogy. Here, paradigms can be used to reveal the essence of a concept or principle and how it can be applied in differing situations. The school, for example, could be used as an analogy for an imaginary state. The headteacher would be seen as the ruler of the state, the teachers as the ministers and the pupils, the ruled. Questions could be posed and issues raised about the state and the relations between the rulers and the ruled. Why and how had the ruler and ministers attained positions of power and influence? What characteristics should they have to maintain their influence? What could the ruled do if they disagreed with the directives of the ruler and ministers? How would they go about changing things? Why would they deem change to be necessary, or what could the motives of it be? How could the ruled effect change, if the ministers were behaving in an unjust manner? An analogy such as this would have limitless potential for allowing pupils to understand the aspects and principles of citizenship in an engaging and relevant manner. Once the analogy has been discussed from a variety of angles and in sufficient depth it could then be applied to real-life situations outside of the school context. The analogy would not only assist in helping them to see the relevance and importance of the issue discussed, but also it would enable them to relate what they had learned to their own lives in an interesting and engaging manner.

Teaching the controversial

So-called 'controversial ideas' have often been excluded from the curriculum, usually because they are considered too personal, such as sex education, or are too contemporary, such as political education, or both. Yet controversial issues already form part of the curriculum in every subject. Citizenship education will invariably increase the number of controversial issues in the curriculum. If everyone in a school thought the same there would be no controversial issues. Thus, an issue in citizenship will be controversial because it will involve value judgements and is contested by others, but people are also divided about what makes an issue controversial. Controversial issues are therefore important to individuals and one can expect passions to rise on the issue. The classroom is an appropriate place to handle controversial issues in a reasonable and fair-minded way, with the emphasis on inquiry rather than indoctrination.

A number of teaching strategies can be employed to assist the inquiry, including brainstorming, debating, arguing, role playing, team work. Discussion is often cited as an ideal way to deal with a controversial issue since it requires the participation of pupils which, with a skilful teacher, ensures a contribution from all. The task of the teacher is to promote the pupils' views and not to expect a consensus of views, but rather to accept a degree of divergence. There will be a degree of divergence because the teacher cannot be entirely neutral in any class discussion for he or she will need to intervene to prevent discussions based on ignorance or loose opinions. The teacher needs to provide stimulating materials for a serious discussion which provides sources and in this way the teacher will feed the discussion. The teacher will also help the discussion by providing different perspectives so that the pupil learns to use evidence-based arguments in order to explore and deepen their understanding of the issues. The teacher effectively should adopt the role of discussion leader. However, he or she will need to ensure that the discussion has been planned, is intellectually rigorous and challenges the pupils. While the pupil has a right to their own point of view the teacher will need to develop intervention strategies – especially knowing when to intervene and what questions to ask. They will need to learn how to focus the discussion in order to avoid superficial coverage of a topic. Pupils should be taught how to be critical of underlying principles, rather than named people – they should learn how to listen and how to understand both sides of an argument and perhaps even be prepared to change their mind when the evidence strongly indicates that they should.

The outcomes from contemporary issues are also difficult to predict, unlike remote issues, so the teacher must dissuade their pupils from adopting premature commitments or positions. The teacher will seek a balanced approach which ensures that as far as possible all aspects of a discussion are covered. Controversy can be planned or arise spontaneously in the classroom. The teacher is not neutral, but needs to cover the views that the pupil will not necessarily have considered. It is this that often leads parents to feel some cause for concern or indeed objection. It is easy for a teacher to present a description and discussion of the main political parties in the classroom, but if they decide to cover such political groups as the National Front then it can cause difficulties. The accusation that teachers indoctrinate is often groundless. Indoctrination is a difficult and complex area with a variety of meanings in the literature. It essentially means that a teacher teaches something as true regardless of evidence and their pupils accept it unquestionably. Crick maintains, however, that 'students have a natural protective scepticism' which secures them against such rabid or insidious indoctrination from incompetent individuals masquerading as teachers. All views must receive fair treatment, but above all pupils need to think about controversial issues if they are to develop as citizens.

Education versus indoctrination

Bias is something that few of us, if any, are free from and while it is legitimate and entirely natural for teachers to have their own commitments it cannot be acceptable for them to teach in a biased way. It may however, be legitimate for them to teach in a committed way in order to change some individual attitudes in the classroom – such as racist or sexist remarks. Society, which is a liberal democracy, is not neutral and expects teachers to promote procedural values which includes applying democratic principles within the community, beginning in the classroom. The ability to deal with bias is taught in a few National Curriculum subjects, particularly in history. Citizenship education teachers will need to develop further a pupil's ability to detect bias in contemporary human activities. In order to teach pupils how to avoid bias it is important that teachers design classroom activities that assist in the detection or identification of:

- the omission of information and alternative points of view in books, films, newspapers, radio, television and other forms of media;
- the deliberate highlighting of certain facts to the exclusion of others;
- the appearance of prejudice and discriminatory practices;
- the creation of 'facts' or 'evidence';
- the use of loaded vocabulary;
- the presentation of value judgements, opinions or views as facts; and
- the avoidance of accepting the significance of contradictory facts.

Pupils need to recognise that all sources are incomplete in themselves or as Bernard Jones (1991: 26) says: 'If education has a legitimate bias, it is towards truth. If teachers have a legitimate bias it must be towards objectivity which seeks the truth. The adoption of strategies and techniques which negate the effect, intended or otherwise, of bias within the class-room, and encourage the students to negate the effect, often intended, of bias from without'. Consequently, teachers need to teach as objectively as possible having due regard for the age, ability and experience of the pupils. However, it is far more likely that you will experience a range of bias, or indeed prejudice, among your pupils than consciously teach anything that is overtly biased.

Teaching the affective domain

Ostensibly there is something of a paradox in the teaching and learning of citizenship: its need for inclusion on the curriculum has arisen as a result of perceived pupil apathy towards both their representative institutions and communities, yet the success of the teaching itself relies upon the active engagement and involvement of the pupils. This presents teachers with a conundrum: how can they ensure the active learning that citizenship demands when they are confronted with essentially indifferent learners? The answer here lies in the teacher's ability to plan and deliver lessons which are imaginative and interesting and which problematise the study of citizenship in a way that engages and involves the students.

The current literature on teaching and learning citizenship is also at pains to stress the need to teach about citizenship by teaching through citizenship. Here, the end of becoming a citizen is achieved in part by the means through which one becomes a citizen. This is stated with clarity in the Citizenship Order itself: 'Teaching should ensure that knowledge and understanding about becoming informed citizens are acquired and applied when developing the skills of enquiry and communication, and participation and responsible action'.

It is not just the content which is important in citizenship; equal prominence is given to the skills required to acquire that content. Indeed, the content of citizenship itself presupposes a certain style in its teaching; one cannot instruct about the importance of rights without allowing individuals to express their opinions. Indeed, there is something of a paradox here, for pupils also have the right *not* to express an opinion. So what is new about this 'style' of teaching that is to be employed? Apart from the emphasis on both skill and content in achieving the ends of citizenship, very little. It is envisaged that teachers will plan lessons which ensure 'active' learning.

Active learning focuses more on what the students are actually 'doing' as opposed to the more vague notion of 'experiencing'. Exactly what it is that students should be 'active' in doing has been suggested in the Citizenship Order. Here, under the headings 'Enquiry and Communication' and 'Participation and Responsible Action', are found verbs which should be of guidance when planning activities and lessons. Pupils should be engaged in activities which allow them to 'research and analyse', 'express and justify' and 'defend and explain'. Activities should also be planned which allow pupils to 'contribute and participate', 'evaluate critically' and 'negotiate' while at the same time acquiring knowledge of citizenship itself. Clearly, then, citizenship education has melded together both skill and content; both have become the end product, unlike in other subjects where debate revolves around either a skills-based approach or the more traditional content-based approach. In citizenship education both have been given equal prominence: citizenship is both knowledge and understanding about active membership of a community and an appreciation of the skills required to be an active member of that community.

Here is a checklist that may be of use in determining what the appropriate skills of citizenship mean in practice and approaches to building them into activities within individual lessons. An interesting way of introducing pupils to the concept of bias is to formulate an analogy. The names of pupils in the class can be used to replace the ones suggested here, allowing for a more active attention on the part of the pupils. Below is a possible example, or method, of introducing pupils to the abstract concept of bias.

Example

A man called Alan has been accused of committing a crime. Three people were present when he committed the crime, but only one person saw what really happened.

Here is a list of the three other people who were there at the time the crime was committed.

1. His best friend, Bill.
2. His worst enemy, Charlie.
3. A person who did not know him, Dave.

Bill, his best friend, told the police that Alan *did not* commit the crime.
Charlie, his worst enemy, told the police that Alan *did* commit the crime.
Dave, the person who did not know Alan, said Alan *did not* commit the crime.

Questions

1. Does Bill have a motive, or reason for saying that Alan committed the crime? Why?
2. Does Charlie have a motive or reason for saying that Alan did not commit the crime? Why?
3. Does Dave have a motive or reason for saying that Alan did not commit the crime? Why?
4. Whose evidence do you believe and why?
5. Whose evidence is most valuable and why?
6. Whose evidence is the least valuable and why? Although it is not as valuable as the other evidence, is it still useful? Why?
7. What do you think happened? Why?

What if

Edward was not there when the crime was supposed to have been committed. He heard from Dave that Alan had not committed the crime.
How reliable would Edward be as a witness? Explain your answer.

Bias and the evidence

Understanding the motive or reason for why an account is recorded can help us to evaluate how reliable and useful that particular piece of evidence is. If the reason for writing is a strong one, we call this bias. Bias means point of view. If there is evidence of strong bias for or against a point, we must try to compare this with all of the known facts and all of the available evidence. This is the only way in which we can come to a worthwhile conclusion. But, just because a piece of evidence is biased, it does not mean to say it is useless. We can find out why a person's judgement was coloured in such a way and how this may have affected their understanding of a situation.

When teaching for citizenship it is important that pupils do not just acquire a lifeless collection of information; activities need to be structured around the information that ensure that they reflect upon their choices and that their behaviour is influenced for the better. What follows is a series of suggestions on teaching a contemporary human rights issue or problem, with the focus on ensuring that pupils move away from a mere acquisition of knowledge toward a reflection upon it which is capable of influencing their behaviour.

Scan the newspapers for a contemporary human rights problem, such as the Indonesian Army's persecution of Christians in East Timor or the lack of civil liberties in Burma. The fact that the problem is a contemporary one should ensure that no claims for relevance need be made. Once you have identified the problem and the pupils have read the article, brainstorm what they already know about the historical background to the issue. This could then be presented on the board as a spider diagram. You could then provide a brief historical background to the problem, highlighting the major issues at stake. To acquire this knowledge, activities such as teacher exposition, timelines or whole-class reading could be employed. But if the teaching is to be effective it needs to be appreciated that this acquisition of knowledge is only the beginning. This knowledge now needs to be used to influence their behaviour. Here the key is to pose a series of questions with prompts or structured answers that are capable of working towards this end. A question could be, for example, what are the possible solutions to the problem and how workable are these solutions? Or, how could a repetition of such a problem be prevented? Once these issues have been discussed it is important to pick out the threads of this particular problem and see what, if anything, they have in common with other related topics or contemporary human rights problems already discussed. Not only does this allow the pupils to make connections, but it also allows them to move beyond the example itself to a consideration of the structural foundations of the problem. When discussing race, for instance, the discussion could move to questions, such as what is a stereotype, what is a scapegoat, who creates them, where, when, why and how? Could this problem happen elsewhere in the world, if not why not and so on.

Having broadened the analysis to include these considerations you could then allow the pupils to reflect upon what they have learnt and how it may impact upon their behaviour. Pose questions such as how has the study of such a problem changed them or how would it influence their future behaviour? What can be done and what should be done to redress the problem and what are the possible or potential consequences of such actions? Indeed, at this stage, teachers could introduce questions of a more general nature, such as what the human rights problem studied reveals about life and about people. The sharper the questioning the more the pupils are forced to think through the problems themselves and reflect upon how it can or should change their behaviour.

Critical thinking

Every pupil has a right to be able to come to their own judgement about something through the exercise of their critical dispositions in making decisions. Every teacher would agree that pupils need to question and use their critical faculties and that teachers should not attempt to do the thinking for the pupil. Teachers of citizenship education therefore need to develop critical thinking in the pupil by placing emphasis on pupils seeing the connectedness of ideas and concepts. This will involve the development of problem-solving skills and the ability to use and apply knowledge. Teachers and pupils therefore need to explore the sensitive issues within citizenship education together which will allow for:

- the development of independence of mind;
- the ability to judge whether the conclusions from an argument follow necessarily;
- being able to have an open mind;
- the ability to organise thought coherently;
- the ability to distinguish between valid and invalid data;
- being able to seek credible sources;
- the ability to grasp the meaning of something at an early stage;
- seeking reasons for something – cause and effect;
- the ability to use evidence impartially;
- being able to analyse an argument;
- being able to make a reasonable evaluation of something; and
- recognising valid generalisations.

Pupils will need to engage with teachers, each other and materials which encourage reflection, discussion, reading, writing, debate, investigation and serious enquiry which aid critical thinking. The teacher needs to plan and prepare for this in order that pupils are exposed to practices in and outside of the classroom which aid rational decision making and which in turn foster critical thinking. A range of teaching methods can be employed to facilitate learning in critical thinking techniques from simulations, role play and information technology to everyday teacher use of question and answers. Pupils should also learn how to be self-critical.

It is well to remember that all forms of commitment, whether in a strong conscious form or a largely unconscious and vague form, affect all teaching. It might also be argued that procedural neutrality approaches to teaching offend against the enthusiasm which good teaching needs. As for ideas of objectivity in teaching, even in teaching the sciences it is now regarded as only possible in part, and in teaching the humanities personal involvement and intuition is accepted as unavoidable and indeed in many cases essential and desirable. In the teaching of citizenship education there will be a need to affirm a critical appreciation of the value of active citizenship. This teaching should nurture in the pupil a desire to accept and make one's own the basic goals of active citizenship. The teacher, in encouraging this positive affirmation of citizenship, will also seek to help sharpen the pupils' critical faculties and develop their personal autonomy.

Conclusion

Teachers of citizenship education need to respect and be responsive to their pupils which will have the benefit of helping pupils with their own self-esteem. The organisation of the school, the classroom atmosphere, the teaching methods adopted and the interaction between teacher and pupils, and between pupils themselves, and the general ethos of the school are all essential elements in planning a teaching and learning strategy in citizenship. So too are the individual experiences, values, beliefs, judgements and prejudices of the pupils. It is from the basis of the school environment and the individual pupil that the teacher attempts to teach the pupil to take a full part in democratic society. However, if pupils are to participate they need to know what it is they think about issues – they need to be equipped to judge events in human life, to understand when something is biased or controversial and to be able to apply their critical thinking in order to make a decision. Teachers and teaching are not neutral and it may be useful to distinguish between teaching and pedagogy as Simon (1999: 406) says:

> Usually, talk about teaching refers to specific strategies and techniques to use in order to meet pre-defined given objectives. However, it is an insufficient base for constituting a practice whose aim is the enhancement of human possibility. What is required is a discourse about practice that references not only what we as educators might actually do; but as well, the social visions such practices might support... Pedagogy is simultaneously about the details of what students might do together and the cultural politics such practice supports. Thus to propose a pedagogy is to propose a political vision.

To enhance human possibility, teachers need to own a vision if they are to move beyond teaching.

Teaching cannot therefore be a neutral process for values are an integral part of teaching which are reflected in how the teachers teach and interact with the pupils. The time spent by pupils in the company of teachers is inevitably formative and, intentionally or not, teachers will most certainly shape the character of pupils. Teachers are also role models and pupils need the example of those who are not indifferent. They need teachers who are full of enthusiasms and commitments in their teaching. In teaching controversial issues teachers must not present one-sided views of political, social or moral issues. Indeed, section 406 of the Education Act 1996 forbids the promotion of partisan political views in the teaching of any subject and also forbids the pursuit of partisan political activities by pupils under the age of 12 in school. If schools do not ensure that their pupils are not offered a balanced presentation or opposing views when teaching controversial issues then anyone can make a formal complaint under the legislation. However, as QCA's *Initial Guidance* (2000: 35) to schools reminds teachers: 'The need for balance [in teaching controversial issues] should not be regarded as inhibiting a clear stand against racism and other forms of discrimination. Our common values require that there are behaviours that we should not tolerate.'

Tasks

TASK 5.1

Attempt a definition of the principles of citizenship.

An approach to the above task may include reference to the following:

a) Rights and Duties
  To what are we entitled and to whom are we obliged?

b) Power and Authority
  How are these entitlements and obligations created and enforced?

c) Identities
  Who is(n't) entitled and who is obliged and why?

d) Representation and Change
  How are our entitlements and obligations represented and changed?

e) Conflict and Conflict Resolution

What happens when there is a conflict or imbalance between our entitlements and our obligations?

How is this imbalance resolved?

Posing questions such as these about the principles of citizenship should help focus the material content of the lessons and add a sense of drive and purpose to the delivery of the lesson itself. Material should be selected that both highlights the question and enables pupils to work towards a satisfactory answer to it.

TASK 5.2

Consider the list below and prioritise three activities which would be most appropriate for the following three areas: teaching controversial issues, understanding bias and developing critical thinking.

Instruction	Brainstorming	Group discussions
Answering questions	Reading	Writing reports
Problem solving	Asking questions	Role playing
Class discussion	Using statistics	Responding to textbooks
Lecturing	Simulation activities	Individual discussion
Observing activity	Information searches	Undertaking experiments
Cross-curricular work	Use of computers	Team teaching
Visiting speakers	Displaying work	Silent, individual work

TASK 5.3

Devise activities that focus on teaching or encouraging the following skills set out in the Citizenship Order:

Research and analysis
- Express and justify
- Defend and explain
- Contribute and participate
- Critical evaluation
- Negotiation

TASK 5.4

Critical thinking

The following is a useful checklist for assessing progress in argument devised by P. J. M. Costello in Education, Culture and Values (2000). Structure an activity which enables the pupil to do a variety of the following points adapted from Costello:

- express a point clearly;
- take a point of view, express an opinion;
- make a personal value statement;
- express a preference;
- give several appropriate examples;
- make comparisons and contrasts;
- use analogy and supposition;
- use persuasive language in giving a variety of appropriate reasons;
- quote and evaluate evidence;
- draw upon own and authoritative experience to support arguments;
- be relevant and logical in structuring, developing and presenting an argument; and
- summarise and take into consideration other arguments or points of view.

CHAPTER 6

Experiential learning in the community

An active citizen… is someone who not only believes in the concept of a democratic society but who is *willing* and *able* to *translate* that *belief* into *action*. Active citizenship is a compound of knowledge, skills and attitudes: knowledge about how society works; the skills needed to participate effectively; and a conviction that active participation is the right of all citizens.

(Education for Active Citizenship – 1989: 7 Australian Government)

Introduction

Most school learning takes place in the classroom and yet for citizenship education it is by no means an ideal learning environment. School teachers realise that there are many contexts for learning and also recognise the growing importance of activity-based learning in and out of school and the need for greater control by pupils over their own learning. Indeed, it could be said that active citizenship implies and even requires *action* on the part of the citizen pupil. The ability to think and act on social and political concerns underpins effective citizenship education. Pupils therefore need to develop active, collaborative and cooperative working patterns in their lives focused on real problems in a real community – what is variously called service learning, community-based learning, community participation, community education or experiential learning. For the purposes of this chapter we will use the term 'experiential learning' to cover most of the activities included in all the other terms listed above. We acknowledge that other terms may be preferred by teachers and refer readers to an excellent summary of the research and literature on school and community involvement found in Dyson and Robson (1999). For us, experiential learning can have an extremely broad or narrow definition depending on what the 'experience' is. We define it as the knowledge, skills and understanding acquired through observation, simulation and/or participation by engagement in activity, reflection and application. It should provide for both the pupils' affective and cognitive development. Experiential learning is therefore about doing something which integrates concrete experiences with reflective observations about the experience. It is essentially about informed participation in communal affairs.

Citizenship education, more generally, is about positive human values which should engender understanding in human beings, prompting them to act in particular ways, especially through offering opportunities to practise political and social responsibility in the community. This cannot be learnt only from books as it must also be based on social practices which all human beings require and should therefore be an essential and integrated element offered by the school curriculum. The aim of experiential learning in the community is to advance and contribute to academic learning together with individual personal development and responsibility. It is about learning for oneself through personal experience and it is already an element in some subjects in the curriculum. It is linked to building strong communities and viewing the pupil as a resource to their communities. There are obviously many kinds of experiential learning in the community. It needs to be planned and executed to create positive opportunities for pupils to develop the range of knowledge, concepts, dispositions and skills to become citizens in a democratic society. It must also form part of their lifelong learning and, above all, the kinds of participation in community encouraged should be more than engaging in good works such as raising money for charity.

John Potter, Director of CSV Education for Citizenship calls experiential learning 'active learning in the community' (ALC). He defines it as an educational method which offers concrete opportunities to pupils to learn new skills and to think critically. He believes it should be incremental, progressing from one year to the next and integral to what is taught in the whole curriculum; he advocates a whole-school approach that responds to the needs in the school and community. He also believes it should be assessed, accredited and celebrated. ALC is clearly more than simply helping out in the community – there need to be outcomes and the pupil must learn. There are also many benefits from such an approach including, among others, giving pupils a sense of purpose, independence, self-understanding and confidence, leadership skills, a sense of belonging and positive personal values. Community Service Volunteers are currently building a database on agencies in the community that schools can turn to together with examples of good practice which it hopes to circulate via the internet. In summary, Potter (1999: 10) defines experiential learning in the following way: 'It is based on a methodology that brings together young people's activities that benefit others with structured curriculum-related opportunities to learn from the experience'.

All of this fits well with communitarian conceptions of citizenship which emphasise that identity and stability of character cannot be realised without the support of a community and therefore there needs to be a contribution from the pupil to their community (Arthur 1999). Indeed, the strongest advocates of 'community service' programmes have been American communitarians who believe it to be an indispensable prerequisite of citizenship education and Etzioni (1995: 113) argues that it is the 'capstone of a student's educational experience' in school. Communitarians advocate mandatory community service programmes in schools because they say volunteer programmes only attract a minority of students. However, few states in the USA have made it mandatory whereas in England there will be a legal obligation on all schools to introduce some form of experiential community learning. Indeed, while the Crick advisory committee on citizenship did not recommend community involvement as a mandatory part of citizenship education it was nevertheless given statutory status by the Secretary of State for Education in the Citizenship Order. Schools are therefore legally obliged to provide some form of community-based learning for every pupil. The advantages of this experiential learning for English schools are outlined by Annette (2000), but almost all the evidence and research findings he uses are from the USA. He also adopts a clear communitarian perspective, borrowed from the USA, emphasising building civic virtue through civic participation.

Objectives

At the end of this chapter you should be able to:

- understand the various forms that experiential learning in the community can take;
- develop a knowledge of group work;
- explore a number of examples of how to manage and teach experiential learning in the community; and
- manage community learning programmes.

Young (1999: 469) has outlined the main obstacles to experiential learning in the community and lists them as:

a) the superiority of subject-based knowledge;
b) the undervaluing of practical knowledge;
c) the priority given to written knowledge as opposed to other forms of presenting knowledge; and
d) the superiority of knowledge acquired by individuals over that developed by groups of pupils working together.

All these obstacles are located within the school curriculum. He argues for an education that gives pupils a sense that they can act in the world, an education which helps create new knowledge and the relevance of school knowledge to everyday problems. Community participation on the part of pupils offers the possibility of fulfilling the vision outlined by Young. Garratt (2000) believes that community participation is predicated on an Aristolean perspective, where the process of becoming habituated through experience in community leads to the development of a virtuous character. He argues that pupils should be exposed to as many experiences as possible in and out of school which encourage positive behaviour. Ruddock and Flutter (2000) also seek to 'create a new order of experience for them [pupils] as active participants'. They recognise that secondary schools offer less responsibility and autonomy than many pupils would be accustomed to in their lives outside of school. All of these educationalists, while recognising the problems associated with experiential learning in community believe that citizenship education offers, through its community dimension, opportunities to develop active citizens. Others, such as Tooley (2000), argue that citizenship education should be learnt out of school. He believes that the State should not intervene in schooling by providing citizenship education as this will lead to greater control over individuals. The authors of this volume, while recognising that education alone cannot bring about the development of active citizens, do not accept his arguments and refer readers to McLaughlin (2000) for a detailed rejection of Tooley's argument.

To help in addressing the needs of the community, CSV defines three types of service, or action that can be implemented. These include, *direct* action, in which the pupils have 'direct contact with the service recipient'; *indirect* action, in which the pupils help an organisation that is responsible for providing a service, but do not have direct contact with the recipient of that service; and *advocacy*, in which the pupils promote or highlight a need to community leaders via the media of letters, articles or press coverage.

The resource identifies three broad categories of community needs. These are the local, the national and the global. For each of these 'communities', the same process outlined above can be used to identify and address the issues that affect them. The materials then deepen into a more profound discussion of the ethics and values that underpin or indeed emerge from such an inquiry. Activities that will enable reflection upon such considerations are also suggested. You should consult the CSV package of resources and materials and choose one or two appropriate activities and follow them through with a class of pupils. Alternatively, devise your own tasks based on the principles outlined above.

Research among student teachers by Voiels (1998: 204) indicates that newly qualified teachers saw 'belonging to' and 'being part of' a community as essential aspects of citizenship. It was found that there was a need for students to understand community from a theoretical perspective, particularly the political and sociological aspects. Hart (1992) offers us a way of understanding this process of becoming part of a community in outlining a model of community participation which he calls the 'participation ladder' and in a summary form it can be described as:

a) pupils understand the community project they are involved in and know its purpose;
b) that they know why they are involved;
c) that they have a meaningful role within the project; and
d) that they have made a free choice to be so involved.

(a), (b) and (c) are necessary before (d) can be reached. Holden and Clough (2000: 20) add a further clarification point in detailing their idea of 'action competent' – in which the pupil is able and ready to participate and can argue, reflect critically and relate his or her opinions and actions to a values framework. They describe this as a values-based participation in community, but do not provide us with how these values are formed in any depth.

A good community participation programme will address the issue of academic relevance by connecting knowledge, skills, values and concepts with accomplishing a meaningful purpose in the school and/or community. Therefore experiential learning is an integral part of school improvement and contributes to this by ensuring that knowledge is gained by the pupil through guided interaction with the community and local environment. It should develop critical-thinking skills which help pupils make evaluations and judgements since community issues and problems cannot always be neatly defined and solved so pupils will also develop problem-solving skills. This should in turn assist pupils to think across the boundaries of traditional curriculum subjects which should help them become more adept at integrating and applying what they are learning. Experiential learning, well planned and executed, allows pupils from a variety of backgrounds and abilities to work together on real problems that provide unity and purpose beyond the classroom. This facilitates inclusion, promotes equity and fosters appreciation of cultural diversity by assisting pupils in relating to others from a wide range of backgrounds and life situations. It will help pupils to value and understand the differences among individuals and communities. The school community itself will change by creating new relationships with the local community which will become increasingly viewed as a positive learning environment which benefits the school. As all members of staff and pupils become participants in the process of experiential learning they develop a personal and collective stake in making something positive happen beyond the walls of the school.

Building a pupil's community participation will obviously entail developing the ability to contact elected officials, to express and voice opinions, to volunteer and become directly involved in a local issue, to be informed about local changes and events, to be interactive with local government services and information and be familiar with the law. Schools will need to consider how they can initiate or further develop any collaborative partnerships they have with local agencies or organisations. Does the school use the local community as a resource to facilitate pupil learning in the community and facilitate involvement of the community in the classroom? A number of questions need to be considered before experiential learning can begin:

- What does community participation or experiential learning mean to the school?
- Does the school have a philosophy of community participation?
- Who should be involved in planning community involvement?
- What will they do?
- What expectations/goals will pupils be expected to attain?
- What is the cost of starting a experiential learning programme?
- Will pupils be helped to become more successful and better citizens as a result of community participation?

- In what ways will experiential learning in community be a support to other school subjects?
- How will the school prepare and train the planning team about experiential learning?
- What are the first few important steps?

Experiential learning through community involvement or participation will naturally take many forms. It can be justified on economic grounds in that it may lead to better and more efficient use of resources when planners consult with the local community. It can strengthen solutions by bringing a variety of perspectives to each issue. It can also assist in developing a mature democracy when the public are involved in decision making. However, community participation should not be equated with simple conceptions of self-help or charitable work or as a substitute for the services that local and national government are obliged to provide. On psychological grounds experiential learning in the community is often justified on the grounds, as Doyal and Gough (1991: 50) say, that 'participation within social life is necessary not only to avoid harm, but more fundamentally to "be human", since identities are formed through interaction with others'. Pupils need to learn and believe that they can have some say over events in their lives and indeed that they can be agents of change in community in helping to shape both their own future as well as that of others. Community participation or learning should be a question of choice on the part of the pupil despite the legal requirement for only then can the conditions for individual freedom be enhanced. This implies that there should also be an unquestioned right of exit from community participation. This will be difficult for schools to arrange, but schools must not compel pupil participation in community projects. Here lies the problem of motivating young people. One possible solution is for the teacher to think about how to develop strategies which encourage pupils to work with each other.

Group work strategies

The teacher obviously needs to structure the learning experiences which take place out of the school. However, before this can be done the teacher will need to understand how to establish groups which are collaborative. Every pupil will need to feel valued and secure so the climate of the group established must be right. Pupils therefore need to be involved in establishing the group and be party to discussing and setting the agenda. Pupils also need to be given and take responsibility for designing, managing and reviewing their own community initiatives. First, the teacher needs to consider how best to establish groups.

In establishing a group teachers need to think about:

- what are the objectives of the group;
- the time scale;
- the size of the group;

- whether the pupils self-select or are required to be in a group;
- whether the pupils know each other;
- how the group is to be led;
- what is the make-up of the group, i.e. gender, etc.; and
- what is the purpose or task of the group.

Asking the pupils to think of all the different groups they are involved in or belong to, the contributions they make to them and the roles they play within them is a good class starting point. The first aim of establishing a group is to encourage the pupils to cooperate with each other. This in itself will, if managed well, help develop a range of social skills including listening to each other and working together to achieve a common goal. The teacher needs to promote and teach the virtue of cooperation by inculcating the idea that it is positive to work together; to know others and care for them; to accept others and assist them; and to build a group in which everyone feels that they are a full member and belong. This exercise in itself can help build community and the self-esteem of the pupils and fosters better social relationships in the school. It may even balance the strong tendency in some school cultures to over-emphasise competition among pupils. Groups can be as small as two pupils and this pairing of pupils can be a non-threatening way to begin. Groups might consist of three or four well-established friends or be made up at random and can even be the whole class. The teacher will need to be sensitive to the context in which they are establishing groups, but ultimately they are seeking pupil interaction across the whole class so they will need to establish clear rules of conduct for these groups and perhaps initially decide the role of each pupil in the groups. A supportive environment must also be established with the pupils taking ownership of the rules. The pupils need to feel accountable for each others' participation in the group and learn that they can do more together than they can do alone.

Another important purpose of using groups is to help each of the members to resolve conflicts that will inevitably arise. The teacher will need to ensure that no one dominates a group and that no one is isolated, embarrassed, frustrated or not respected. In addition, the pupils will need to learn that they must take account of each other's point of view when they work out a reasonable and fair solution to any problem. The teacher's role is to intervene when necessary, but as the group becomes more effective then the teacher should increase the responsibility of pupils to solve their own problems without adult assistance. The teacher is in effect attempting to make themselves redundant in terms of the functioning of the group. If pupils are to develop responsibility they need to *have* responsibility and group work assists this because it requires a learning-by-doing approach on the part of each pupil. They will come to recognise the value of group work in that it can be creative, enjoyable, constructive and draw on the ideas and experiences of everyone in the group. Resolving conflict may even encourage pupils to be more caring of each other – it forms an essential part of the participatory citizenship education.

Working in and with the local community pupils will learn about the kinds of values and dispositions that are necessary for effective participation in society. They will also gain knowledge of the nature of community itself. The Education Reform Act 1988 requires that all teachers help prepare their pupils for 'the opportunities, responsibilities and experiences of adult life'. Community Service Volunteers has extensive experience in the area of community involvement and has listed five citizenship competencies for experiential learning which are worth listing here. They are:

- to work in a variety of group settings;
- to identify and evaluate the values and ethics of self and others in the community;
- to recognise, appreciate and support vital elements of the local community;
- to gather and evaluate data necessary to effect positive change; and
- to implement effective decision-making and problem-solving strategies.

All of these competencies need to be integrated into the academic school curriculum and CSV also lists four components which must be present to provide a quality experience for pupils. First, *preparation*, which is concerned with orientating the pupils for action. Second, *action*, which is the hands-on experience. Third, *reflection*, which is developing critical skills. Finally, *celebration*, which is due recognition for the pupils' efforts and learning (CSV 2000: 13). The teacher must involve the local community to avoid misunderstanding. Schools already have considerable experience of work-related education, including organising work experience for their pupils. The development of GNVQs and NVQs have also increased the relevance of the school curriculum to the world of work. Experiential learning in the community complements work experience. The introduction of experiential learning in citizenship education will require the school to listen to the needs of the local community and to incorporate some of those needs into its curriculum planning. Pupils will need to recognise common ground between the aims of the school and the local community if they are to have a more coherent view of their own social development. The OFSTED *Handbook for the Inspection of Schools* (1993) will no doubt be revised to take account of citizenship education for it already has evaluation criteria for 'links with parents, agencies and other institutions'. Teachers will need appropriate training and professional development to promote effective experiential learning activities.

The implications of experiential learning in the community-based evaluations that have been conducted by CSV (Potter 1999: 17ff) indicate that it:

- promotes all three strands of citizenship education;
- requires careful implementation which is linked with the mission of the school and related to the curriculum;
- does not require a prescribed curriculum, but needs a curriculum framework with clear outcomes;
- requires training for teachers and well-designed materials;
- promotes overall school improvement; and
- develops pupils' basic social skills.

Other research indicates that it has the potential to increase examination results and attendance rates together with promoting positive pupil changes such as pupils accepting responsibility for their own learning and improving their social skills in relationships with others (CSV 2000: 13).

Planning

The *Initial Guidance* to schools on citizenship education issued by the QCA (2000: 16–17) states that schools should involve families in the planning of active community involvement. They should also consider developing community links with: other schools; environmental groups; civic, religious, charitable and voluntary groups; as well as with local employers and councils. There are also youth services, industry and commerce and interagency cooperation which schools need to make connections with. These should be the focus of community involvement so that pupils are provided with suitable learning challenges within appropriate contexts. This will enable the school to offer a variety of different community project types. The school will also need to incorporate experiential learning in the community into its overall development plan which is linked into other aspects of the curriculum. This will also require school support through adequate administrative assistance. The following points need to be considered when preparing a plan for a community project:

- What are the aims and objectives of the project? Will the project meet the learning and developmental needs of the pupils?
- What attitudes, skills, understandings and dispositions are to be fostered?
- What are the key tasks? Are they understood by all involved?
- What are the teaching and learning strategies to be deployed? Do they allow the pupils to reflect on their experiences, talk through them and share them with each other?
- Are their community placements involved and for what duration? Teachers will need to negotiate each placement with the pupils and decide whether it will be for half-a-day each week or a longer period.
- What resources are required? Will the pupils need to travel and will they require equipment to carry out their tasks?
- How are the pupils to be assessed and monitored? The teacher may consider the use of diaries to provide feedback on the experience through debriefings and follow-ups. Is the assessment method used linked with the school assessment policy?
- How will the project be evaluated? By whom and when?
- Who are the community partners involved? The partners of the project in the community need to know what is expected and they must be willing to fully participate. Will they visit the school to meet the pupils?
- Are there health and safety issues? Are any permissions necessary from parents?
- What is the timetable for implementation? Is there a schedule of key dates?

- What are the INSET needs of the staff who are to be involved? Roles need to be clear.
- Who will manage and coordinate the project? Whoever manages the projects must be able to raise awareness among the school staff about the purposes of this type of learning and how it assists general school learning.
- Are there any qualifications associated with the project? Teachers might consider qualifications from private organisations listed in chapter four or the new qualifications being offered by the examination boards at GCSE level.

Managing a community participation project for secondary school pupils will be a time-consuming and complex activity for any teacher. Local education authorities could assist here by providing the school with guidance on community involvement. It might even be suggested that this type of education might be better provided if it were externally resourced and led. A number of local education authorities have provided some excellent guidelines on citizenship education, particularly on community involvement. Birmingham, for example, has established benchmarks for citizenship in its publication *Success for Everyone* (see Lloyd 2000) which enable schools to review their provision for citizenship by matching their present provision and practice against the ideal. They provide a progression from minimum standards all schools should subscribe to, and are described as: *emergent*, perceived as a secure foundation; *established*, as continuing to develop provision; and *advanced*, as excellence in one or more aspects of provision. The Birmingham model is clearly locked into school improvement and covers the areas of leadership, management and organisation, creating the environment, teaching and learning, staff development, collective review and parental and community involvement. Birmingham Education Authority is clearly at the forefront of developments in this area and has set aside 2002 as the Year of Citizenship. Hampshire Education Authority is another authority which provides schools with guidelines on initiating and developing community contacts, school–community partnerships, sharing good practice – by means of case studies, developing a school council, involving children as active citizens, an outline management framework for implementing citizenship education – and all of this is freely available to all on the web at http://www.hants.gove.uk/education/ngfl/pseweb/. Hampshire also provides planning guidelines for assisting schools implementing the Citizenship Order by producing *The Citizenship Education Planning Framework* which is available for £20 from Hampshire County Council. Both these education authorities, together with some others, provide schools with expert assistance to make effective use of the range of community contacts available to them.

The citizenship coordinator will have a multiplicity of roles which will include planning and negotiating, getting to know the local community, helping to bring people together, clarifying goals and being able to decide what is needed, together with good interpersonal skills and the ability to work within teams. They will need to be experienced at developing community networks and partnerships and be able to develop a community-orientated curriculum. They will also need to be able to manage placements in the community and provide monitoring and supervision. They will need to define the relationship between the school and community so that the contributions of community groups is understood by all involved. Above all they will have to decide whether a particular project is a task-centred activity which fulfils the objectives of the programme. Indeed, clarifying objectives for experiential learning in community as part of a citizenship education programme will be one of the first tasks of the coordinator. These objectives should include:

- increasing awareness of social, political and moral issues;
- encouraging participation as a way of giving greater control over resources and the decision-making process;
- working with others to influence the course of change;
- ensuring better service delivery and more comprehensive provision;
- increasing pupils' capacity to respond positively to their communities;
- increasing pupils' capacity to discover, define, pursue and achieve common goals together; and
- advancing lifelong learning.

The coordinator will require an adequate support structure within the school which involves both resources and a satisfactory level of funding to promote development. A member of the senior management team will also need to have an overview and responsibility for citizenship education and ensure that there are clear lines of communication between staff and the citizenship coordinator.

Methods:

There are many techniques which a school can adopt to promote the community involvement requirements contained in the Citizenship Order. Table 6.1 provides only some of the types of activity which many schools have already used:

Table 6.1

Cooperative learning:	pupils work together to achieve common goals
Internship:	supervised practical application of previously studied theory
Service learning:	pupils work as volunteers with social agencies
Mentoring:	the use of an advisor to guide the pupil
Simulation:	pupil-centred activities that challenge
Projects:	pupil is given a specific community project to do
Outward Bound:	wilderness adventures
Team building:	working together
Field study:	study in a practical setting
Shadowing:	observational experience of a career

Assessment

The evaluation of experiential learning is also vital at the end of each placement. In planning the placement each pupil should be encouraged to state what they think they will gain from the experience – a *learning plan*. In so doing they should describe their objectives – what they will learn, not what they will do. How will it enhance their personal and academic development? What will they do to realise their objectives? How will they self-assess their progress? Their personal goals are described here. Assessment should assess the progress they have made in achieving their objectives – not for the work they do *per se*. Eisner (1993: 226–32) presents a framework for evaluation consisting of 'eight criteria in search of practice' which offer a possible route for the evaluation of experiential learning in community. According to Eisner evaluation tasks should:

1. reflect real-world needs, by increasing the pupils' problem-solving abilities and ability to construe meaning;
2. reveal how pupils solve problems, not just the final answer, since reasoning determines pupils' ability to transfer learning;
3. reflect values of the intellectual community from which the tasks are derived, thus providing a context for learning and enhancing retention, meaning and aesthetic appreciation;
4. not be limited to solo performances, since much of life requires an ability to work in cooperation with others;
5. allow more than one way to do things or more than one answer to a question, since real-life situations rarely have only one correct solution;
6. promote transference by presenting tasks that require pupils to adapt intelligently modifiable learning tools;
7. require pupils to display an understanding of the whole, not just the parts; and
8. allow pupils to choose a form of response with which they are comfortable.

A portfolio approach may be the best way forward as it provides a flexible format which allows for a variety of evidence to be built up by the pupils themselves.

Conclusion

Community education is a term which is notoriously ambiguous and open to different interpretations. Many educationalists and teachers believe that experience in learning is as, if not more important than the content of what is taught. Active experiential learning aims to acquire social, political and personal skills which are essential to the practice as well as the understanding of citizenship. Experiential learning in the community provides pupils with concrete opportunities to participate with others in serving the public. It presents schools with a powerful way of enhancing their pupils' learning by developing an effective range of social skills. The progress of pupils in citizenship needs to be recorded through a variety of means and they will need to learn how to gather their own evidence of progress towards the attainment target. This means that teachers need to support pupils in reviewing and recording their own evidence which can be used by the teacher to compile the annual reports on citizenship which will be required. However, the circumstances for active community involvement need to be present in the local community for it to work. The school cannot create these itself and they will only happen if local and national government truly encourage participation and involve the public in this process. Schools need to respond imaginatively to the new opportunities that experiential learning offers. Above all, schools will need to be committed and be able to adopt good principles for community involvement and participation which follow through into good practice.

Experiential learning cannot remain as a 'peripheral' activity of the school and it appears to us that this type of learning is often best addressed outside the formal structures of the school because the aims and values promoted are more congruent with the processes being learned. Many schools have successfully involved themselves in this area and found to their surprise that the community can also become the teacher. However, we know from the very limited studies that have been done that service learning or community involvement has not been a priority of many English schools (UNICEF 2001: 8). Indeed, some believe that faith in community experiential learning schemes is perhaps overly optimistic for schools. It is also the case that mere emphasis by a school on community participation will not necessarily ensure that pupils will participate responsibly. Pupils may be motivated by self-interest rather than being public-spirited, confirming McIntyre's (1999) fear of 'How to Seem Virtuous Without Actually Being So'.

Tasks

TASK 6.1

a) Compile a database of all the various community organisations and institutions which might be useful in offering placements for experiential learning. Ensure that you include contact names, addresses and telephone numbers. Check with the LEA on whether or not there is a policy advisor on community education. The LEA may also be able to offer suggestions on compiling a list of local voluntary organisations.

b) What are the advantages of experiential learning in the community? Does it help motivate pupils? Is it more fun to do?

c) Following on from task 1.3 (Audit of Citizenship Education), consider in more detail what is already being done in your school in terms of community involvement. What contribution is being made by community organisations? What resources and funding is accessed by the school? What do other subjects areas do in terms of their links with the community – e.g. music, PE, theatre studies and media, etc?

TASK 6.2

In 2000 the CSV Education for Citizenship organisation, in connection with Deutsche Bank, published a resource package with book and materials for teachers. The package includes many excellent practical suggestions for teaching citizenship. It is particularly strong on the community and experiential aspects of citizenship. It structures experiential learning into the following stages and assumes that the following questions have been asked.

Devise an activity which addresses each of the questions in the task.

Definition of communities

- What is the community?
- To which community do we belong?

Identification of the needs of a community

- How do we identify the needs of our community?
- What are the needs of our community?
- Who will help us in addressing the needs of our community?
- What will be our contribution to addressing such needs?

Implementation of the proposed 'solutions'

- How will we implement our plans?

Evaluation of the 'solutions'

- What did we achieve in this project?
- What was rewarding or unrewarding about it?

Reflection

- How can we consolidate what has been achieved?
- How can we address what has not been achieved?

Celebration

- How do we celebrate our achievements?

TASK 6.3

Read the following case study to your class and then divide them into groups and provide each member of the group with a copy of the case study.

The Case Study:

Sycamore Road is a busy street with narrow lanes, but it is heavily used by car drivers using it as a short-cut between two main roads. There is a large primary school on the street and parents find it difficult to park when bringing or collecting their children. Crossing the road is extremely difficult for pupils, especially as some cars travel at over 30 mph. The local council and the Police have conducted one or two surveys and have concluded that it is not a severe problem. However, parents and local people are very concerned about both the traffic and the noise.

Each group member must take time to think about how they feel about the case study. The group should then organise itself in such a way that every member can be listened to. The group should then discuss the following key questions about how the group would take their next steps:

- Is there a problem? If yes, what is it?
- What are the reasons for the problem?
- What do we as a group want to achieve?
- How can we go about it?
- Who needs to be involved?

In reporting back to the rest of the class the group needs to be questioned about how realistic their plans are and about who would lead it and see it through. Are they offering a meaningful contribution to the community and how would they develop partnerships with the parents and local people?

TASK 6.4

Using the Hampshire Education Authority website, access the section on 'consid-erations for initiating and developing community contacts'. After reading this section prepare a scheme of work for a community project involving Key Stage 4 pupils. Ensure that the following questions are fully answered:

What is the theme of the project?

What support is required?

What resources are needed?

Are visitors required in the classroom before the project starts?

Are pupils to be taken off site?

What off-site regulations must you comply with?

Who can provide you with contacts in the community?

What support is available from:
a) your school;
b) the local education authority;
c) voluntary organisations?

CHAPTER 7

Resources and citizenship education

David Leddington

Introduction

There is a growing range of resources now available for citizenship education, which offers teachers guidance and information in introducing the subject to schools. There are, of course, both human resources and material resources. Many national and international organisations provide materials for citizenship education that include: reports, statistical data, yearbooks, commentaries and other school materials for teaching. The National Curriculum for Citizenship states that pupils should be taught to 'think about topical political, spiritual, moral, social and cultural issues, problems and events by analysing information and its sources, including ICT-based sources'. However, you will need to be careful in the selection and use of some of these materials in the classroom. The following provides a brief review of the main resources easily available for teaching citizenship education, which is intended to be indicative and exemplary rather than exhaustive in scope. The forthcoming book on *Resources for the Teaching of Citizenship in the Secondary School*, edited by Leddington and Tudor, will provide a selection of teachers' materials and resources that will give further guidance on how to resource citizenship education along the lines indicated in figure 7.1.

Objectives

At the end of this chapter you will have:

- an overview of the resources available for introducing citizenship education in schools;
- an overview of some of the community organisations which might assist you with citizenship education in school; and
- a critical approach to the use of resources in citizenship.

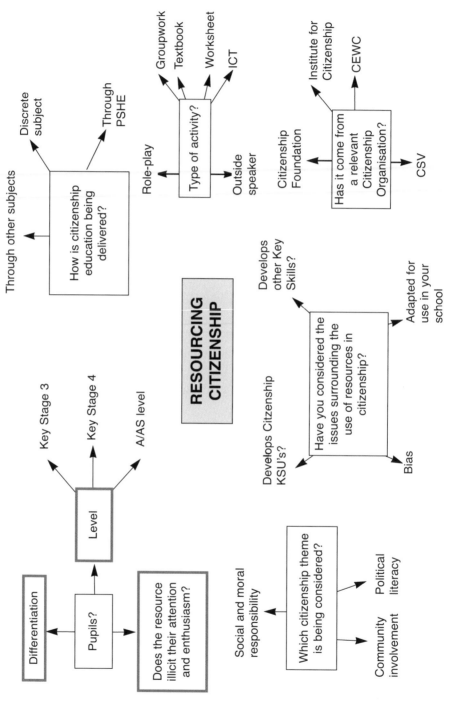

Figure 7.1 Points that need to be considered when resourcing citizenship education

As discussed in chapter five, an important consideration when planning to resource any task or activity for citizenship education is the issue of bias. Citizenship education will contain teaching about controversial areas or topics, such as the Holocaust or racism. It is therefore important that any teachers of these areas or topics are aware of the sensitive issues that are obviously contained within them. Certain organisations which provide resources and material on citizenship education have their own agenda and so you must be aware of this fact when using and selecting materials for use in the classroom which may have a particular slant or bias. As suggested by the QCA, in order to avoid bias on controversial issues teachers will resist:

- highlighting a particular selection of facts or items of evidence, thereby giving them greater importance than other equally relevant information
- presenting information as if not open to alternative interpretation
- setting themselves up as the sole authority
- presenting opinions and value judgements on facts
- giving an account of others' views, instead of real sources
- revealing their own preferences
- implying preferences by not opening up discussion
- neglecting a challenging consensus of opinion.

(QCA 1998: 58, para. 10.9)

This has implications for the teaching style or method used and the resources employed for that task or activity. To avoid selecting and using material that is biased it is advised that you consult the National Grid for Learning (NGfL) website for guidance on the range of materials and resources available and who created them. Generally, resources created by one of the 'Coalition for Citizenship' organisations – the Institute for Citizenship, the Citizenship Foundation, the Council for Education in World Citizenship, the Community Service Volunteers, the Centre for Citizenship Studies in Education, the Hansard Society and the Foundation for Citizenship – are recommended. Many of them have now established links with publishers and are increasingly producing textbooks, CD-ROMS and other resources for citizenship education. These should prove challenging, stimulating and differentiated while meeting the National Curriculum requirements and also ensuring a balanced approach is followed. These resources are becoming increasingly available with many of them scheduled for release by the end of 2001.

Organisations that provide guidance on resources

There are a host of key organisations that can be contacted for further information regarding citizenship education. In particular these organisations are providing constructive support for schools and teachers of citizenship education by creating a range of resources that can be used in the classroom. The QCA regularly publishes updates for guidance on the development of citizenship education, which are available on www.qca.org.uk. Furthermore, the QCA also provides the programmes of study for citizenship online at www.nc.uk.net. In the summer 2001 the QCA will also send support materials to schools. These will include schemes of work allowing schools to teach these programmes of study in various ways. It will also support and illustrate how citizenship can be taught as a discrete subject, through other subjects and through other whole-school activities. It will include:

- examples of good practice, e.g. community involvement;
- guidance on curriculum planning; and
- reference to useful resource materials for schools.

The National Grid for Learning website www.ngfl.gov.uk is constantly being developed and provides links to other relevant sites. One of these linked sites that is particularly useful when considering the suitability of resources is the Hampshire Grid for Learning (www.hants.gov.uk/education/ngfl/pseweb). This website, created by the Hampshire PSE team and the Hampshire Inspection and Advisory Service, provides a very useful guide to citizenship education. It includes recommended links to relevant citizenship organisations, resources and examples of good practice for teachers, pupils and parents. It has also created a *Citizenship Education Planning Framework* pack that is available to support the development of citizenship education in schools. It has been designed to ensure that schools plan their citizenship education programmes within a coherent and active learning framework. The materials in this pack provides:

- a focus on the nature of citizenship;
- the importance of citizenship in preparing young people for adult life;
- how this might be integrated into the curriculum and school life; and
- how other agencies and members of society might work with schools to achieve this.

The planning framework therefore offers ideas that help identify ways that all teachers could contribute to the development of citizenship education and ensure an integrated and coherent approach at an initial stage. It is suggested that the pack should act as a 'springboard' for ideas and not be prescriptive – i.e. it should be flexibly and imaginatively interpreted for use in each individual school.

Resourcing the key strands of citizenship education

The three main strands of citizenship education – social and moral responsibility, community involvement and political literacy – need to be remembered when considering resources. When planning to teach citizenship education it is important that the task or session is based on one of these three main strands. Indeed, one or more strands may be included. Each strand may, at some point, require a different type of approach, a different teaching style and therefore different resources. However, you must always ensure that the task set or lesson is always suitably planned and prepared for. Publishers are producing resources and materials for use in the teaching and learning of citizenship and democracy education, for example Pearson Publishing have produced teacher packs, student guidebooks and downloadable 'epacks'. Some groups, including the 'Coalition for Citizenship' organisations, have also developed support packs, advice and resources that allow you to plan and resource the teaching of all three strands of citizenship education. *Understanding Citizenship,* developed by the Citizenship Foundation, is a progressive course for Key Stage 3 citizenship. Through a series of three students' books and one teacher's book, it has been developed to provide a straightforward and up-to-date means of teaching the statutory orders for citizenship. Building on the interests of young people, it uses imaginative and interesting activities that encourage an understanding of their rights and responsibilities, and should stimulate critical-thinking skills of discussion and enquiry. It forms a sound basis for classroom discussions, project work and wider activities in school and the local community.

The Institute for Citizenship has identified a number of topical issues which teachers and pupils feel are important and at the same time would motivate pupils through their *Key Stage 3 Pilot Project*. Using these topics they have incorporated the elements of the citizenship Key Stage 3 programme of study into the lessons. This has led to a varied and flexible set of resources. Topics to date include:

- refugees;
- young people and the criminal justice system;
- sustainable development; and
- e-commerce.

For each topic the institute has worked in partnership with relevant professional organisations to ensure the resources benefit from specialist input. These topics are being piloted by the schools and revised in the light of their feedback and advice. Schools are also tailoring the resources to meet their own needs and developing exciting projects which extend the learning taking place in class and provide opportunities for wider participation. For example, year 7 students from Islington Arts and Media School were involved in a dance project with students from Rosemary School, and Fairfield High School ran a special citizenship week of activities. All these examples of successful projects will be evaluated and disseminated by the institute and made available to teachers. It is envisaged that the curriculum material generated by the pilot will be used in a variety of ways. Available termly from May 2001 will be curriculum projects developed in cooperation with other specialist organisations. These approach the national requirements for citizenship through a range of perspectives and issues. A teacher starter pack that draws upon the experiences of the pilot schools will also be available from May 2001. This will provide a summary of relevant requirements, guidance and background issues as well as practical advice and examples of how to implement citizenship education. These will be complemented by a NFER evaluation (National Foundation for Education Research) of the work in the pilot schools. This will be available from September 2001. The report of the first phase is available now and summarises the research undertaken by NFER, on behalf of the Institute for Citizenship. This aimed to understand how much of the citizenship programme of study was being delivered at the beginning of the project, what teachers felt were the main challenges and the views of students about what they would like to see as part of their citizenship education.

Using the findings of this project the institute is developing, with the publishers Nelson Thornes, a series of textbooks covering all of the elements of the Key Stage 3 National Curriculum in a local, national and global context. These books, and the supporting material for teachers, are being developed through close collaboration with experienced teachers and reflect a focus on practical classroom activities to develop knowledge, understanding and skills across the key stage. They will be published during 2001–2. A CD-ROM, using pictures to explore citizenship issues, is also being developed and will be available from September 2001. This is being developed from work already undertaken by several schools for students with learning difficulties, but should be flexible enough to meet the needs of a wider group in mainstream schools.

The Council for Education in World Citizenship (CEWC) also produces a very relevant pack of materials, resources and ideas for the three main strands of citizenship education – the *Towards Citizenship* support pack. The full pack contains teachers' notes, though a sample pack is available online. This pack gives teachers examples of criterion-referenced learning programmes in citizenship and PSHE and is designed to encourage teamwork while rewarding individual effort. It also provides a further suggested resource list and other useful contacts. The pack contains a number of resources for the following areas that have been designed for use in the classroom:

- rights and responsibilities;
- the community;
- health and safety;
- independent living;
- economic and industrial affairs;
- careers;
- the environment; and
- international understanding.

Some of these are considered later in this chapter. They are particularly useful as some of them may be downloaded from their website. This should allow you to adapt them or combine them into lessons that also develop pupils' use of ICT in the classroom.

The Children's Society (www.the-childrens-society.org.uk) is another organisation which has produced a resource pack that addresses the main strands of citizenship education. *Education for Citizenship – A Resource Pack for Key Stage 3* is a resource pack that can be used flexibly and creatively by the teachers of citizenship. It was published in 1991 and so predates the new Citizenship Orders. However, the resources have already been piloted and used extensively in some schools, though mainly through PSHE sessions. The activities range from classroom-based activities that can be used in individual lessons to longer term projects that could be used to allow pupils to conduct work and research in the local community. They can therefore be adapted and developed for however your school plans to deliver citizenship education. The main areas covered include: young people and the law; homes and homelessness; families and care; poverty; and young people's rights. By focusing on these areas the aims of the pack are broadly similar to the aims of the National Curriculum for Citizenship. They include heightening awareness and understanding of important social issues among young people; encouraging discussion; promoting personal and social responsibility; and encouraging young people to fully participate in the community and society's institutions. The teacher of citizenship could therefore apply or adapt these resources to fulfil and develop pupils' knowledge, skills and understanding of the citizenship curriculum.

These resources and materials effectively consider the three main strands of citizenship education. However, there are also a wide range of other resources that can be used to effectively resource each of the particular strands, as described under the following headings.

Social and moral responsibilty

Within this strand of citizenship education pupils should learn self-confidence and social and moral behaviour, including towards each other and towards those in authority. There are many resources presently available for this area, many of which overlap with PSHE or 'whole-school' materials. Pearson Publishing already publishes photocopiable materials that support PSHE and citizenship. The Citizenship Foundation has also produced resources that link PSHE with citizenship. Examples include its *Charity Matters* pack, the *Understand the Law* guide, *Human Rights ImpACT* and *Young Citizen's Passport*. The *Understand the Law* resource includes four volumes of active learning units that cover all aspects of the law as it affects young people at home, school, work, shopping and in personal relationships. It was specifically written by non-specialists in secondary PSHE courses. The *Young Citizen's Passport (Human Rights Act Edition)* is also a guide to the law that now includes a chapter dedicated to the Human Rights Act 1998. As well as a valuable personal resource, the *Young Citizen's Passport* is an excellent basis for citizenship and PSHE teaching during the later years of secondary education. *Human Rights ImpACT* is a booklet outlining how UK citizens will be affected by the incorporation of the European Convention on Human Rights into British Law. However, an important distinction between citizenship and PSHE in secondary schools is that citizenship education in Key Stages 3 and 4 requires that diversity and the importance of tolerance in a democratic society is taught. You may therefore need to adapt some of these existing materials to comply with the Citizenship Orders. Examples of textbooks that directly tackle this strand of social and moral responsibility in citizenship education are *Human Rights* and *The Citizen and the Law* from Collins' educational series *Citizenship in Focus* for Key Stage 4 pupils. *Human Rights* tackles the issues of what human rights are; the time for action; child slavery; euthanasia; asylum seekers; and the rights of women. *The Citizen and the Law* textbook tackles issues such as why we need laws; civil law and criminal law; crime; the police; the courts; and prisons. Both of these books provide a useful and structured approach for pupils learning about these key issues within citizenship education. By using these or a similar series of books, you can match the topic and activity with the knowledge, skills and understanding that should be developed in pupils at this level. Like many of the published resources that are becoming available they tackle more than one theme of citizenship, in this case the emphasis being on social and moral responsibility while also making links with political literacy.

The Citizenship Foundation is also in the process of creating new resources specifically designed for the National Curriculum for Citizenship and which focus on the social and moral responsibility theme of citizenship education. *Citizenship for All* is a resource book covering many personal and social issues, particularly with less academic secondary students in mind, though much is ideal for mixed ability groups. Knowledge and understanding are interwoven with material designed to develop attitudes and values. *Good Thinking: Education for Citizenship and Moral Responsibility* contains three courses of study for Key Stages 3, 4 and '5', introducing students to moral ideas, language and debate within a framework of citizenship and public morality. The course builds progressively through the key stages from simple situations and dilemmas to complex social problems.

A topic that will be explored through citizenship education in many schools is the Holocaust. The first Holocaust Memorial Day took place on 27 January 2001 and will be repeated each year. This is the anniversary of the liberation of Auschwitz-Birkenau. It has been created for reflective and also educational purposes. The focus of the day is to raise awareness and develop understanding of the relevance of the Holocaust in order to learn the lessons from it. Studying it will provide pupils of citizenship a powerful reminder of the dangers of racism. Among its aims are:

- to recognise that the Holocaust was a tragically defining episode in the 20th century, a crisis for European civilisation and a universal catastrophe for humanity;
- to provide a national mark of respect for all victims of Nazi persecution; and
- to raise awareness and understanding of the events of the Holocaust.

Furthermore, it attempts to ensure the development of pupils' understanding of their social and moral responsibly within citizenship education by reflecting on similar issues; promoting a democratic and tolerant society; opposing racism, anti-Semitism and victim-isation; and by highlighting the values of a tolerant and diverse society with equal rights and responsibilities for all its citizens. Further information on this can be obtained from www.holocaustmemorialday.gov.uk. It has been complemented by an education pack published by the DfEE (2000). This pack, *Remembering Genocides, Lessons for the Future*, is an invaluable guide for a school considering the Holocaust. The pack contains a variety of appropriate resources for assemblies and activities that could be used in 'follow-up' sessions on the issues raised. The materials are age related and can be used on a whole school basis with supporting follow-up activities. Other organisations that produce reports and materials on the issue of tolerance include the Runnymede Trust (www.runnymedetrust.org). This organisation has created a number of resources that consider diversity in a multi-cultural society. Not only has it published reports considering issues concerning racism and antisemitism, but also issues surrounding attitudes of young people towards Europe. It is a useful website to consider for a range of social and moral responsibility issues.

Community involvement

Within this theme pupils should learn how to become actively and helpfully involved in the life and concerns of their neighbourhood and communities. This should include learning through community involvement and service. Pupils should therefore develop their active and responsible participation in their communities. Resourcing this theme will require an investigation into how pupils may involve themselves in their community including the school, the wider community, local issues and local organisations. Informa-tion and guidance for developing pupils' participation skills can be obtained from Schools Councils UK (www.schoolscouncils.org), an organisation that obviously promotes the development of school and class councils. The organisation provides a range of teachers' packs and videos to assist the development of an effective school council. Furthermore, the site provides useful information on how using any pupils' forum in the classroom can be beneficial in developing their involvement in their community and reinforcing their understanding of the process of democracy.

The Community Service Volunteers (CSV) has some excellent advice on how to develop pupils' citizenship education by promoting their active participation in their community. It produces a wide variety of resources that should be considered. The *Discov-ering Citizenship* pack has been designed to be relevant for teachers of citizenship educa-tion with links to PSHE and other subjects. It should provide experiential opportunities for students to develop their 'skills for life' through active learning in the community. It is split into a teaching toolkit and students guide. The toolkit provides a methodology of active learning in the community reinforced by a plan for teachers. This includes lesson plans and possible role plays. The guide allows students to log their progress – gathering evidence and data and responding to questions raised by the scheme. It can also contribute towards award schemes such as The Duke of Edinburgh's Award and Trident. The *Absolutely No Limits* pack provides a guide for the issues regarding volunteering in schools. It describes how schools could design community-volunteering schemes to meet their needs. It provides practical guidance, resources and a framework for evaluation for staff working with volunteers. Materials for training volunteers and volunteer mentors are also included in this pack. The *Passport for Life* pack is similar to a number of schemes now being used by secondary schools. It contains a teacher's handbook, pupil passports, posters and other materials necessary for this scheme that attempts to develop pupils' sense of involvement and inclusion within the school and wider community. Community Service Volunteers have also collaborated with Barclays Bank in its *New Futures* scheme that aims to promote citizenship by providing awards for schools. Further information can be obtained from www.community.barclays.co.uk.

Political literacy

Within this strand pupils should learn about the institutions, practices, issues and problems of democratic life. They should also learn how responsible citizens could make themselves effective in public life at local, regional, national and even international level.

A key point to consider when developing pupils' political literacy is that all societies, including democratic ones, have individuals within them that promote racism and other prejudices. Democratic societies will only develop if the rights of all its peoples are treated equally and they are active participants. Therefore when resourcing this strand, pupils' understanding of diversity and the importance of active participation within a democratic framework should be developed.

There are numerous further examples of resources and textbooks that tackle this strand, either dealing with citizenship education in particular, such as the *Citizenship in Focus* series, or via related subject textbooks, such as *This is History! – King John* published by John Murray.

The *Citizenship in Focus* series (Foster 2000), previously mentioned, provides a useful example of textbooks and teacher resource packs which are focused solely on citizenship. The series textbooks that are relevant to the theme of developing pupils' political literacy are *Democracy in Action* and *Global Concerns*. The *Democracy in Action* textbook deals with the following issues: democracy; Britain's system of government; being a Member of Parliament; the Houses of Commons and Lords; elections and the case for possible reform; political parties; local government; and the European Union. *Global Concerns* tackles issues that include: what power is; what globalisation is; the United Nations; world trade and Third World debt; population; world hunger; arms and weapons; the media; the internet;

and the environment. Both of these books are good examples of the textbooks currently being produced by a number of publishers which will assist you in ensuring that pupils develop their citizenship knowledge, skills and understanding at Key Stages 3 and 4.

The *This is History* textbook also attempts to develop pupils' citizenship knowledge, skills and understanding but via a related subject, history. There are strong links to be made from many subjects presently on the curriculum – including English, geography and history – and there are explicit links outlined in the National Curriculum. This textbook links pupils' historical understanding of the developments in British history to their understanding of democracy; in this case, how the changing relationship between monarch, parliament and people during the Middle Ages shows how democracy in Britain gradually developed. This increasing range of textbooks contain history topics, all presented with a citizenship perspective. They are a good example of some of the new subject textbooks becoming available. The teacher's packs also contain a range of notes and lesson ideas and are cross-referenced to the relevant citizenship knowledge, skills and understanding so that you can compare how both subjects are being covered.

A very effective website that should be used from the outset when researching and planning how to resource the political literacy strand of citizenship education is the Houses of Parliament own site (www.parliament.uk). This website contains a particularly useful section – 'Explore Parliament' (www.explore.parliament.uk) which offers information, resources and online activities pertaining to schools. It also contains information about Parliament's Education Unit; with details on how to use the online activities; guidance on how these activities could be used in teaching citizenship education (as well as other parts of the curriculum) and links to other useful websites. The resources and links it contains will assist in the planning and resourcing of citizenship lessons. In particular, there are downloadable resources on:

- Parliamentary elections;
- The House of Commons;
- The House of Lords;
- Parliament and Government;
- how laws are made; and
- Parliamentary debates.

The interactive activities on this site include a quiz on Politics and Citizenship and an enquiry-based activity that allows pupils to discover who their MP is. The site can also be used to arrange educational visits to the Houses of Parliament.

For further information on the role of Parliament and the process of democracy, and when resourcing the political literacy strand of citizenship education the Hansard Society should also be considered. They organise 'mock elections' on a regular basis which schools can participate in to provide an active and enjoyable means to introduce young people to the democratic process in this country. They have support from the DfEE and

BBC to ensure that the project follows the elements and requirements of the National Curriculum for citizenship. In collaboration with the BBC and the Corporation of London they have also produced a CD-ROM on *The Parliament and Government* which allows pupils to investigate: Parliament; public opinion; the Constitution; Europe; the City of London; the wheels of Government; political parties; and elections. This resource provides a multimedia method of presenting information regarding British democracy that should prove popular and effective with students.

Charter 88 (www.charter88.org.uk) focuses on issues regarding electoral reform and political freedom. It produces a guide, *The Charter 21 pack* available from www.citizen21.org.uk/pack, that deals with these issues. It can provide useful sources of information and act as a basis for discussion and debate within a classroom environment. The pack includes booklets that tackle issues such as citizenship, a bill of rights, freedom of information, the reform of parliament, voting reform and the decentralisation of power. The website also provides useful further information on each of these areas with resources (including videos, CD-ROMS and photo-packs), links to other relevant websites and related events. A CD-ROM that would complement this area of discussion has also been created by the Citizenship Foundation. *A House for the Future – A Teacher's Guide* has been available to schools since January 2000 based on the report on the reform of the House of Lords by the Royal Commission. A pamphlet was produced by the Citizenship Foundation for use alongside the CD-ROM, but can be used alone as an aid to discussion of issues relating to the House of Lords in general.

Websites of the other British political assemblies

The following websites provide further information on the other national political assemblies in the United Kingdom. They all contain information about that assembly; the membership of that assembly; debates; and publications.

www.assembly.wales.gov.uk – the website of the Welsh National Assembly
www.ni-assembly.gov.uk – the website of the Northern Ireland Assembly
www.scottish.parliament.uk – the website of the Scottish Parliament

Other political organisation websites

www.royal.gov.uk – this website is the official website of the British Monarchy. It contains information on the role of the Monarch in the British system of government and its historical development. It also contains information on the accessation, coronation and succession of the Monarch.

www.pm.gov.uk – this website contains information about the latest developments in government as well as a virtual tour of No 10 Downing Street.

www.europarl.eu.int and www.europa.eu.int – both of these websites contain useful information about the European Parliament and European Union.

www.un.org – this contains information about the work and historical development of the United Nations. Furthermore, it also contains information about the United Nations Charter and the Universal Declaration of Human Rights.

Websites of relevant political parties

www.tory.org.uk – the website of the Conservative Party
www.greenparty.org.uk – the website of the Green Party
www.labour.org.uk – the website of the Labour Party
www.libdems.org.uk – the website of the Liberal Democrat Party
www.plaidcymru.org – the website of the Welsh National Party, Plaid Cymru
www.snp.org.uk – the website of the Scottish National Party (SNP)
www.scotsocialistparty.org – the website of the Scottish Socialist Party
www.sinnfein.ie – the website of the Irish Republican Party, Sinn Fein
www.sdlp.ie – the website of the Social, Democratic and Labour Party
www.independenceuk.org.uk – the website of the UK Independence Party
www.ukup.org – the website of the United Kingdom Unionist Party
www.dup.org.uk – the website of the Democratic Unionist Party
www.uup.org – the website of the Ulster Unionist Party

Creating your own resources

When planning to resource citizenship education you should always evaluate the suitability of the resources available for citizenship education. Schools are currently preparing to implement the statutory requirement of teaching citizenship education. To meet this demand publishers are producing a great variety of resources and materials to support the teaching and learning of citizenship in secondary schools. You will need to consider whether these are suitable for the particular needs of your school's community and possibly adapt them. Though textbooks, or any of the resources mentioned in this chapter, will always remain important resources for teachers it will be vital to supplement them through creating your own worksheets, card-sort exercise, newspapers and other resources. These should contain relevant information and extracts from primary sources. Teaching citizenship education involves learning about community involvement and developing pupils' active participation in their own communities. As each school community, and the communities in which they are based, are different so you will have to adapt the possible ideas and resources mentioned. As Hughes (2000) states: 'Tailor made resources are more likely to be effective than off-the-shelf purchases'. A flexible and imaginative approach is therefore essential when resourcing citizenship education. It will require you to create your own materials and ideas that match the needs of your school community.

Worksheets

Worksheets will be widely used by many teachers of citizenship education to supplement the other resources that they will possess. The production of a variety of high-quality worksheets will be a vital aid to your teaching. However, it is important as with any worksheet that they enhance, support and give structure to pupils' learning and understanding of citizenship. A number of tips, especially when using worksheets, can be used to ensure that all pupils are included in the National Curriculum of Citizenship.

Presentation

The resource used should seize the pupils' attention. That implies that they should be clearly presented – preferably word-processed. It should have a clear and relevant title and the visual quality and layout must also be very good. Any pictures used should be clear and should remain so even if photocopied. Lower ability pupils may benefit from a high ratio of picture to print; though at the same time you must ensure that they are fully included in the lesson and 'stretched' by the activity. Instructions in worksheets should be clear and simple.

Language

The language used is very important in citizenship education, especially when considering the development of pupils' political literacy. When introducing a new term ensure that is fully and clearly explained to avoid confusion. Wherever possible use short, simple words in short sentences.

Content

Education should demand effort and stretch the pupil. Ensure pupils are learning rather than just being occupied. However, asking for too much too soon should be avoided. Choose exciting examples or lively accounts to illustrate themes and concepts.

Exercise of skills

Use a variety of teaching approaches, regularly, to enthuse the pupil and increase their confidence. Any alternative teaching strategy employed to develop their understanding of either community involvement, social and moral responsibility or political literacy may need to be fully explained with instructions provided on an information sheet. The activities that then follow should also be clearly explained.

Differentiation

When resourcing citizenship education it will be important to realise that the pupils you will be teaching will be of a variety of ages and abilities. To ensure that all of them are included in the task and develop from it, any worksheet or resource should be differentiated. Introductory tasks should aim to encourage all students to attempt them while extension tasks should be provided for the more able.

Lloyd-Jones ([1985]1995) provides a series of nine questions that can be used by the teacher of citizenship to create better worksheets. These are summarised in Arthur, Hadyn, Arthur and Hunt (1997) and are replicated below.

Are the worksheets:

- part of a planned, balanced and coherent course; and
- written in language, which is easily understood?

Do they:

- provide opportunities for group work and class discussion;
- require pupils to use a variety of sources and resources;
- ask for a variety of responses, including both oral and written;
- cater for the needs of all levels of ability in the class;
- provide for progression and continuity in learning;
- give clear information and unambiguous instructions; and
- avoid pointless exercises such as blank filling-in or colouring?

Newspapers

Another type of resource that will prove invaluable to the teacher of citizenship are newspapers. As citizenship education may reflect topics that are in the current newspapers then they should be explored and used in the lesson. You should consider constructing your own newspaper articles based on current issues, which would lead to discussion within the classroom. Examples of how this can be done are available from the Hampshire Grid for Learning website (www.hants.gov.uk/education/ngfl/pseweb). It provides useful advice on how newspapers can be created and how they can be used as a resource for the citizenship classroom. As it states: 'the advent of the digital camera, coupled with an increasing range of computer software and hardware has made the production of a newspaper a much more realistic proposition than it once was'. The use and production of a newspaper could even evolve into a teaching strategy that would involve and enthuse all the students. It would also develop their understanding and appreciation of the importance of 'free speech' in a democratic society. To begin to use newspapers as a resource it is important that you first observe the techniques of layout, style and other conventions. This website will soon be displaying a support pack that is being developed for schools that are considering creating a newspaper that can be used as part of the learning opportunities for citizenship. Further examples can also be found and downloaded from the Children's Express website (www.childrens-express.org.uk) and *The Guardian*'s educational site (www.educationunlimited.co.uk).

Tasks

TASK 7. 1

An important aspect within the social and moral strand of citizenship education is the issue of the environment. Use this quiz, amended from CEWC's Towards Citizenship study pack, to debate the issues raised and develop pupils' social and moral understanding.

Global warming quiz

The questions are designed to get you thinking about the issues. You may not agree with all the answers given. Some experts would challenge them.
Circle the answer you believe is correct.

1. Global Warming is related to:

    a)   the hole in the ozone layer;
    b)   nuclear fuel;
    c)   the Greenhouse effect.

2. Temperatures:

    a)   are increasing;
    b)   are decreasing;
    c)   stay the same.

3. Sea levels are:

    a)   rising;
    b)   falling;
    c)   staying the same.

4. The problem is getting worse because of:

a)   CFCs in the atmosphere;
b)   gaseous emissions from car exhausts;
c)   oil spillage in the oceans.

5. Global warming has accelerated:

a)   over the last 20 years;
b)   since the industrial revolution in the 18th century;
c)   since the last ice age.

6. As the world warms up:

a)   there will be more volcanic eruptions;
b)   there will be more cereal food production;
c)   there will be reduced rainfall in some areas.

7. Global warming is particularly affecting:

a)   the Brazilian rainforest;
b)   the Sahara Desert;
c)   the Arctic Circle.

8. Planting more trees would:

a)   reduce global warming;
b)   increase global warming;
c)   have no effect on global warming.

9. The country which produces the most carbon dioxide is:

a)   India, because of the population;
b)   America, because of its lifestyle;
c)   Britain, because of the number of cars in a small area.

10. The area most affected by the greenhouse effect will be:

a)   the most developed countries;
b)   the less developed countries;
c)   all countries.

Answers 1. c; 2. a; 3. a; 4. b; 5. a; 6. c; 7. c; 8. a; 9. b; 10. c

TASK 7.2

Use this example of a resource, adapted from CEWC's Towards Citizenship study pack, to investigate pupils' awareness of their community and local authorities.

1. What is the difference between local and national government?

a) Find out which council(s) and authorities you live within?
b) Which political party is currently in control of that council and authority?

Consider the following services provided by the public sector:

1. The police   3. Public housing
2. The army   4. Street cleaning

a) Which of these services are provided by central, national government and which does local government provide?
b) Why is this the case?

TASK 7.3

As one of the key strands of citizenship education is community involvement, use this planning grid to consider how you could initiate and develop community contacts and the possible issues of resourcing.

Possible Questions	Resourcing Issues
What am I going to teach?	Are there resources readily available? Do I need to create new resources?
What community support is available to me?	Consult the CSV and other relevant websites for guidance
Do I want specialists speaking in the classroom on certain topics?	Consider using history, geography, English, RE or PSHE specialists

Also consider speakers from outside school
- police
- local councils
- MPs
- Citizens Advice Bureau

- local charities
- interest groups

Do I want to take pupils off-site?
Consider the school's off-site regulations
Consider useful local sites
- courts
- council offices
- museums
- government agencies
- church education groups
- health services

TASK 7.4

Using this questionnaire, adapted from CEWC's Towards Citizenship pack, investigate your pupils' political literacy and awareness.

Question	Responses
What is Parliament?	
What is an MP?	
Name your local MP	
What is the House of Commons?	
What is the House of Lords?	
What is the Government?	
Who chooses the Government?	
Name the Prime Minister?	
What is a General Election?	
What are the main Political Parties?	

TASK 7.5

Resources audit

Speak to the citizenship coordinator in the school. Ask what is already being done, i.e. identify where citizenship education takes place in the school; and the contribution made by subjects and/or PSHE. Investigate the range of resources that are available. Consider their suitability. Are they:
• well presented?
• broad and balanced in content?
• up to date?
• challenging and stimulating?
• differentiated?

TASK 7.6

Creating resources: newspapers, magazines and television

As citizenship education considers the values, rights and learning about democracy a valuable source of resources that can be used in the teaching of citizenship will come from issues arising from current affairs. Therefore, continually scan through newspapers or current affair magazines and cut out any articles that would be useful in your teaching. Similarly, consider television listings and make use of any relevant programmes that focus on relevant citizenship issues.

TASK 7.7

Matching activities with resources

The following list, summarised from the Hampshire Grid for Learning website, contains a list of various pupils' possible learning strengths with related activities. Consider the different styles and activities and then consider how they may be resourced. Existing resources may complement many of the activities but you will need to create new resources for others.

Learning style and strengths	Possible activities	Resources
Practical Works well alone Knows how to find information Gets things done on time Organises time well and has time for other things Reads instructions carefully Doesn't get distracted	• research • quizzes • carousel • conducting interviews – visitor experience • matching activities • using newspapers/ printed material • drama strategies	
Logical Organises facts and materials well Sees links between ideas Likes to understand Curious, and enjoys problems Works things out on paper Precise and thorough A good critic	• problem-solving activities • quizzes, word searches, questionnaires, check lists • data collection • carrying out surveys • interpreting data • circle time • problem page	

Learning style and strengths	Possible activities	Resources
Enthusiastic Gets totally involved when interested Works well with other people Writes freely Likes taking risks Works quickly Asks questions or volunteers Learns by talking	• engaging with visitors • debates/creative writing • designing leaflets • card sorts • role play, simulations and hot seating • ice breakers • circle time	
Imaginative Comes up with creative solutions Can see the total picture quickly Unhurried, doesn't get into a flap Comes up with creative solutions to issues/problems Shares ideas Presents work in novel ways	• case studies • responding to visual/oral stimulus • dilemmas • model making • brainstorming • using literature • buzz groups	

CHAPTER 8

Assessing citizenship education

Ruth Tudor

Introduction

The main purpose of assessment in citizenship education, as in other areas of learning, is to improve learning and make progress through the use of feedback. An important part of the challenge of citizenship assessment, therefore, is to find effective means of giving feedback so that all young people make real progress within citizenship education in all its aspects. Another important purpose of assessment is to recognise progression and achievement, including for the purpose of certification and for accountability. Part of the challenge of citizenship assessment will be to support meaningful and valid assessment of achievement and attainment in areas such as whole-school ethos, pupil participation, collaboration, cooperation, self-awareness and self-evaluation. Citizenship assessment is a potentially difficult area because of both how we currently think about assessment and because of the nature of citizenship education. How can we assess an area that requires the active participation of the learner as a citizen and as part of a community, taking responsibility for and reflecting on their own progress, and in an area of education which engages directly with values, beliefs and emotions?

Objectives

At the end of this chapter you will have:

- considered the purposes of assessing citizenship and the importance of using assessment methods fit for these purposes;
- reflected on the nature of citizenship and the implications of its characteristics for citizenship assessment;
- considered how to use assessment to enable progression in citizenship education to take place;

- considered how to use assessment to make judgements about achievement and progression in citizenship education;
- understood the particular challenges involved in accrediting achievement and attainment in citizenship education; and
- appreciated that citizenship assessment and evaluation will involve a wide range of assessors and the implications of this for schools and communities.

National requirements and developments

The statutory requirements for the assessment of citizenship education is the same as for all non-core National Curriculum subjects:

Key Stages 1 and 2

At Key Stages 1 and 2, citizenship education, together with PHSE, forms part of the non-statutory framework. There is no requirement to teach either citizenship or PHSE and no requirement to assess. However, there is an expectation that schools will record and report the progress of each pupil in these learning areas and that parents will have access to these reports.

Key Stage 3

At Key Stage 3 there is a statutory requirement for teacher assessment in citizenship education from August 2002 when it is introduced as a National Curriculum subject. Teacher assessment is about assessing, recording and reporting on progress during the key stage as well as summarising achievement at the end of the key stage. Teachers will make their end-of-key-stage assessments in relation to a single attainment target for citizenship education. It consists of an end-of-key-stage description for Key Stage 3 and an end-of-key-stage description for Key Stage 4. End-of-key-stage descriptions specify the type and range of performance that most pupils are expected to demonstrate during the key stage. Teachers should use the descriptions to help judge how well pupil attainment fits with expectation. The expectation at end of Key Stage 3 is broadly equivalent to levels 5/6 of other National Curriculum subjects. In subjects with end-of-key-stage descriptions, teachers reach a judgement by using evidence of attainment and achievement over time, including written, practical and oral work. This judgement must be reported to parents/carers at the end of the key stage. However, there is no requirement for schools to collect summary data of teacher assessments in citizenship education although evidence of achievement must be kept by schools.

The end-of-Key-Stage 3 description of the attainment target in citizenship education states:

pupils have a broad knowledge and understanding of the topical events they study; the rights, responsibilities and duties of citizens; the role of the voluntary sector; forms of government; provision of public services; and the criminal and legal systems. They show how the public gets information and how opinion is formed and expressed, including through the media. They show understanding of how and why changes take place in society. Pupils take part in school and community-based activities, demonstrating personal and group responsibility in their attitudes to themselves and others.

(QCA 1999)

Key Stage 4

There is a statutory requirement to teach the programme of study in citizenship education at Key Stage 4 from August 2002 but no requirement to assess. Schools, therefore, will be free to assess citizenship in the way that best suits them. Teachers can use the end-of-key-stage description for Key Stage 4, which forms part of the attainment target in citizenship, to make a judgement on pupil attainment during and at the end of the key stage. The end-of-Key-Stage 4 description of the attainment target in citizenship education states:

Pupils have a comprehensive knowledge and understanding of the topical events they study; the rights, responsibilities and duties of citizens; the role of the voluntary sector; forms of government; and the criminal and civil justice, legal and economic systems. They obtain and use different kinds of information, including the media, to form and express an opinion. They evaluate the effectiveness of different ways of bringing about change at different levels of society. Pupils take part effectively in school and community-based activities, showing a willingness and commitment to evaluate such activities critically. They demonstrate personal and group responsibility in their attitudes to themselves and others.

(QCA 1999).

Inspection by OFSTED

From November 2000, primary schools will be inspected to find evidence of the implementation on non-statutory guidelines for citizenship at Key Stages 1 and 2.

In secondary schools, until September 2002, inspectors will continue to comment on aspects of citizenship education under sections 2 and 4 of the framework as they do at present. They will also be encouraged to look for evidence of preparation for the implementation of citizenship as a statutory part of the National Curriculum. From September 2002, inspectors will seek evidence of citizenship as a separate subject under section 10 of the Inspection Framework.

Short Course GCSE in Citizenship Studies

Although there is no requirement to assess at key stage 4, qualifications and certificates are being developed. In January and February 2001 the QCA consulted on draft criteria for a Short Course GCSE in Citizenship Studies. When the criteria have been finalised, they will provide a set of rules and principles to be used by awarding bodies to develop specifications for qualifications under this title.

Citizenship assessment: the main issues

> We aim at no less than a change in the political culture of this country both nationally and locally: for people to think of themselves as active citizens, willing, able and equipped to have an influence in public life and with the critical capacities to weigh evidence before speaking and acting; to build on and to extend radically to young people the best in existing traditions of community involvement and public service, and to make them individually confident in finding new forms of involvement and acting among themselves.
>
> (QCA 1998)

This passage above expresses the innovative and radical nature of citizenship education as it is intended to be realised within schools and colleges in England from August 2002. What distinguishes citizenship education from other areas of current learning is its emphasis on the *participation and active involvement of all learners* within the learning and assessment process. Citizenship education, as expressed in the Crick Report and in the programmes of study for both Key Stages 3 and 4 set out in the Citizenship Order is not simply about knowing and understanding but is about knowing and understanding through doing and being.

As the programmes of study state: 'Teachers should ensure that knowledge and understanding about becoming informed citizens are acquired and applied when developing skills of enquiry and communication, and participation and responsible action'. Pupils will become more informed and responsible as citizens while taking action as citizens. The citizenship programme of study requires pupils to participate, to take action, to reflect, to think critically, to negotiate. It promotes learning that is based on experience and in which the agenda is set in collaboration with the learner. It is about changing learners so that they are enabled to be responsible and informed citizens who use their knowledge, understanding and skills to contribute to and to change society. It may not be helpful, therefore, to see citizenship education as an 'additional' or 'separate' subject within the National Curriculum but rather as an education for skills, qualities and dispositions that will underpin, support and feed into all curriculum areas. Some of these models of citizenship education have been addressed in chapter two.

Citizenship education will not happen in isolated classrooms but will form part of whole-school practice and ethos. Assessment and evaluation will need to take place – not just of individual pupil performance but of the mechanisms by which the school actively involves all its pupils, enabling them to take real responsibility within their school and the wider community. At present, schools are being encouraged to evaluate critically their contribution to and relationship with their communities as well as being encouraged to actively involve pupils in school management and decision making. Such approaches could lead to a radical change in the relationship between pupil, school and community.

One of the greatest challenges of citizenship assessment will be how to assess progress and achievement in the vital participatory aspect of citizenship education. Will there be a tendency to assess those things that are more familiar and easier to measure, such as knowledge and understanding, at the expense of the more complex participatory elements? There is evidence that assessment has a significant impact on teaching and learning styles. If knowledge and understanding are assessed while development and practice of skills are neglected, this in turn will affect what is valued within schools and classrooms, the choice of teaching and learning styles and whole-school ethos.

The citizenship programmes of study require pupils to take responsibility for their own progress and achievements. Pupils will need skills in assessing their own progress in order to improve their performance in citizenship education and in gathering evidence of their progress and achievements throughout the key stages. Teachers will need to share ownership of the assessment process with pupils. They may also need to involve others – including community partners, learning mentors, other colleagues – as assessors. Schools will need to support quality assessment by all who are involved in citizenship, negotiating assessment methods with others.

Teachers working within a multicultural, liberal society, may feel uncomfortable assessing – and therefore judging – performance that engages directly with values, beliefs and feelings. Poor-quality assessment that focuses on judging a pupil's attitudes and beliefs or those of their family, community and cultural group, rather than assessing their progress in awareness of and understanding of values would distort the aims of citizenship education and could discriminate against particular groups of learners on the grounds of race, gender, disability or sexual orientation. Similarly, pupils must not be judged for their feelings and emotions but rather for the progress they make in emotional literacy, for example, pupil disposition and ability to reflect on and understand their own feelings and those of others. It is unlikely to be appropriate, therefore, to use a model of assessment which sees the teacher as imparting knowledge and understanding and assessing pupil work on the grounds of whether it is 'correct' or 'incorrect'. Instead models will need to be developed and used that enable qualitative judgements to be made against multiple criteria. The emphasis in feedback and in summarising achievement should be on individual progress and mastery not comparison with others.

The programmes of study for citizenship are broad, diverse and flexible. This flexibility and breadth is crucial in order for schools and colleges to be able to develop provision for citizenship education which is appropriate for their respective community and school cultures. How can national assessment models and guidance on assessment respond to and cater for this diversity, flexibility and breadth? At the same time national models and guidance will need to ensure balanced coverage of the different and varied aspects of the citizenship programmes of study. In particular, what resources will be available for enhancing consistency in teacher assessment at Key Stage 3 and what mechanisms will be used to ensure comparability across any awards that are developed for use at Key Stage 4 and beyond to post-16.

Teacher expertise in citizenship will have a powerful impact on the quality of assessment. Teachers cannot assess constructs that they do not understand. In order to elicit best pupil performance, teachers will need to set quality tasks and questions within an appropriate context. This point will be as relevant for formal summative assessment as for formative assessment. Awarding bodies that offer qualifications in citizenship will need to set high standards of good practice in both internal and external examination components.

Other important issues are raised by the apparent intention to accredit citizenship education with certificates and qualifications. If citizenship education is about developing knowledge, understanding, skills, qualities and dispositions that underlie National Curriculum subjects and qualifications, is it appropriate to have a discrete qualification in citizenship in the same way as it is in, for example, history, science, art? In addition, the assessment techniques of any qualification, including GCSE, will have an impact on teaching and learning styles. In relation to citizenship education, this could make discrete and subject-based rather than a whole-school learning experience less innovative and flexible than it is intended to be. How can we ensure that the impact of a GCSE in 'Citizenship Studies' will not be to narrow the experiences of learners and lose the spirit and vision of citizenship education as it is intended to be? The need to provide qualifications in citizenship education is not self-evident and the implications of doing so should be considered carefully. The nature of citizenship education means that it is equally relevant and meaningful for *all* pupils. Any assessment method will need to enable all pupils to make progress and have their achievements recognised. In relation to accrediting citizenship, however, there is a tension between citizenship as an entitlement of *all* and the nature of qualifications, such as GCSE, which differentiate between candidates using grade criteria. How can this tension be overcome so that pupils are not put in the position of 'failing' citizenship or of not being given the opportunity to enter a qualification in the first place?

The nature of citizenship education as intended in the report and programmes of study will challenge the pedagogy of many within education. In relation to assessment, it will – for some practitioners and others with influence – require new ways of thinking about both how schools enable pupils to make progress and how and why their achievements are recognised.

Why assess citizenship education?

A clear sense of the purpose of the assessment is required before schools and teachers plan how to assess citizenship education. Effective assessment in citizenship will, as in other learning areas, enable pupils to both make progress (often known as formative assessment) and demonstrate achievement (often known as summative assessment). It is arguable that these purposes cannot be effectively achieved without the participation of the learner. In citizenship education, however, the participation of the learner within the assessment process should be central.

According to Sadler (1989) formative assessment is concerned with how judgements about pupil performance can be used to inform and improve their performance so that real progress is made. Pupils need to know about their performance in order to make improvements. They need to know what improvements they can make or need to make and how to achieve this. If they are making progress, pupils will feel motivated to achieve. Similarly, schools and teachers can use assessments to plan more effectively for the needs of all their pupils and can change their plans in response to assessment outcomes.

Sadler (1989) contrasts this to summative assessment that is concerned with summarising the achievements of pupils, usually at the end of a course, and often for purposes of certification. Summative assessment, as it is usually practised, does not necessarily require the participation of the learner. In citizenship assessment, however, pupils are required to reflect on and review their progress and achievements as part of the summative assessment. Summative assessment in citizenship education will, therefore, need to include a wider range of assessment techniques, approaches and assessors than are currently used by many practitioners.

Assessment can also be done in order to provide evidence of progression and achievement for purposes of accountability. Assessment could, therefore, be used to inform on and celebrate with others, including parents and community partners, pupil progress and achievement in citizenship education. Care will need to be taken, however, that assessment for accountability which involves comparisons being made between the performance of different schools does not distort curriculum provision in citizenship by emphasising consistency and reliability at the expense of validity. There is another, perhaps less obvious reason, which is that teachers assess pupils all the time informally and unselfconsciously. If assessments are occurring all the time irrespective of intent then the assessment needs to be thoughtful, self-conscious, deliberate and productive. This may be especially pertinent to citizenship education, which is in part concerned with values and feelings.

Planning formative assessment in citizenship education

The main purpose of formative assessment is to improve learning. So-called 'formative assessment' occurs when pupils are able to use assessments to make progress. Feedback and self-monitoring or self-assessment are key elements of formative assessment. It is the quality of the feedback – that is, the quality of the interactions which take place within the classroom between teacher and pupil, pupil and peers – as well as the ability of the pupil to reflect.

Although the 'assessor' is usually viewed as the teacher – the emphasis on reflection, responsibility and participation within citizenship education means there is a need to recognise pupils themselves as well as their peers and community partners as assessors. In order for pupils to be involved effectively in citizenship assessment, they need to have a clear sense of what they are aiming at and how a particular learning experience might enable them to demonstrate progress and achievement. Sharing learning objectives with pupils is essential in order to involve them effectively in their own learning. However, the language used in learning objectives is not always or usually appropriate for pupils.

The nature of citizenship education is such that pupils will begin their programmes of study with their current understandings of moral, social and political issues. Progression in citizenship education is about building on these current understandings and assessment of this progression will be crucial. Progression in these areas, however, is not necessarily well understood or commonly practised. The extent to which progression is achieved depends upon careful planning of learning, including assessment. Learning objectives and assessment criteria must clearly show how progress can be achieved. A focus on assessment for progression helps to ensure feedback is ongoing and connected to feedback on progress in other pieces of work.

Assessment criteria (what we will be looking for) should be shared with pupils. They can be helped to understand what the criteria mean by sharing with them the work of a peer or group of peers. Pupils could be encouraged in citizenship to assess their achievements and those of their peers in relation to the assessment criteria. They could be given opportunities to try out different strategies that might be used to close the gap. In this way pupils gain a greater awareness of their own preferred learning styles and that some approaches might work better for them than others.

In developing assessment criteria that show pupils what the assessor is looking for and enable progression to take place, teachers will be guided by the attainment target and end-of-key-stage descriptions. They will need to develop precise, clear and context-specific assessment criteria rather than trying to assess pupils against statements taken from the attainment target. The attainment target is not intended to be used, in itself, as criteria for specific learning activities but instead gives a broad and holistic description of expectations of attainment by the end of a key stage.

Citizenship assessment methods will need to be capable of assessing learning experiences that have a broad spectrum of learning outcomes. Citizenship education is not about knowing 'right' or 'wrong' answers but, on the contrary, is about participating, becoming active learners, developing moral reasoning, developing thinking skills, ability to collaborate with others and so on. It has, therefore, a complex set of learning outcomes that include assessing process as well as outcome. Pupils will need to learn skills that enable them to evaluate their own performance, especially during the process of production and in relation to the learning objectives. For example, are you achieving the objectives? How are you doing this? Why are you finding it difficult to do? (McCallum 2000).

If progress is to be made, the pupil themselves must understand how they can judge their own work and how to improve their own performance. Pupils need to be taught how to assess themselves and opportunities will need to be planned for reflecting on progress and achievements. Pupils need to be given time and guidance in how to solve problems. These opportunities to develop self-assessment skills and dispositions should form part of the scheme of work. The success of such an approach to assessment depends in part on the quality of relationships within the classroom. Trust and self-esteem of pupils (and teachers) will need to be sufficiently high to take risks, try out different solutions, experiment, 'fail' and admit problems. Pupils need to know that if they make a 'mistake' while trying out different strategies for achieving their learning objective, they will not be penalised but instead rewarded for how they reflect on and use that learning experience in order to make progress in the future.

The need to be a reflective, self-aware and responsible learner is a requirement of the citizenship programme of study. Effective feedback will enable pupils to internalise formative assessment, to reflect on their progress in relation to learning intentions and assessment criteria and to become responsible for their own progression and achievements. Or in other words, a shift should occur between 'telling pupils how to improve' and 'pupils seeing for themselves what they need to do to improve'. Feedback is most effective when it focuses on the task and is given while it is still useful and relevant to the pupil. Feedback should confirm what is being achieved and identify what needs to be improved. Evidence suggests oral feedback is more effective than written and, therefore, the quality of ongoing conversations between pupil and assessor about progress is very important. Pupils should be able to use feedback to find their own solutions to problems rather than being given the solutions. Pupils also need to know how to get help with their learning. They should be rewarded for taking responsibility for getting help to make progress. This ability to identify need and get help for that need is a useful learning strategy which is not always recognised and rewarded within school education although it is seen as useful at work.

Planning summative assessment in citizenship education

Summative assessment in citizenship education at both Key Stages 3 and 4 will need to reflect the breadth of the citizenship programmes of study, including its participatory aspects. The key to effective practice will be the extent to which pupils are involved in the assessment process, including reflecting on and reviewing progress in a broad range of areas and collecting evidence of their achievements, which reflects this breadth and diversity. Portfolios, diaries, video tapes, self-assessment sheets and ICT, will enable pupils both to share responsibility for reviewing and recording progress and achievements during the key stage as well as reflecting the variety and richness of their learning experiences.

Moderation could be used to support better quality assessment and enhance the consistency and dependability of statutory teacher assessment at the end of Key Stage 3. Moderation supports high-quality assessment by getting teachers to talk about the assessment criteria used to make a judgement and by sharing ideas about assessment methods and opportunities. Sharing good practice should enable teachers to use a broader range of assessment methods – a broad range will be needed to assess all the varied aspects of citizenship effectively.

Both for purposes of formative and summative assessment, it is likely that teachers will need to work with each other and other assessors, particularly community partners. Teachers will need to support quality assessment from their partners by making sure that learning objectives and assessment criteria are designed collaboratively and arise out of the strengths and expertise of their community partners. Effective feedback between community partners and pupils can be supported with interview schedules and assessment sheets.

It is likely that pupils will generate evidence of progression in citizenship throughout the curriculum. If pupils have a high understanding and ownership of the objectives of citizenship, they will be able to take a degree of responsibility for identifying progression in citizenship in a wide range of subject areas and gathering evidence for their own portfolios. Whatever approach is taken, teachers and pupils will need clear learning objectives and assessment criteria for aspects of citizenship being developed within individual subjects.

Why record and report assessment in citizenship?

Recording and reporting assessment in citizenship will support pupil discussion of their progress with others, including learning mentors, community partners, peers and parents, as well as providing evidence of progress and achievement for teachers and pupils to make a summative assessment of progression and achievement by the end of a key stage.

In addition, recording and reporting assessment in citizenship will enable achievements both within and outside the school to be recognised and celebrated and make it possible to hold schools and teachers accountable for the quality of the citizenship education they are providing. Such evidence can be used by schools when evaluating the quality of their citizenship provision, enabling schools and teachers to identify patterns of achievement over time in knowledge, understanding and skills and to respond appropriately by amending and adapting learning experiences.

It is likely that schools may consider the use of a portfolio approach to help collect evidence of progress and achievement in citizenship. A portfolio system places the responsibility for recording evidence on the learner rather than the teacher. It can, therefore, be a useful tool for helping them manage their own learning, bringing benefits throughout their National Curriculum subjects and developing skills and qualities for adult life. Pupils will need guidance in how to gather evidence. They will need to know the range of skills that their portfolio must demonstrate as well as the knowledge and understanding acquired. Pupils will need to know the assessment criteria against which their portfolio will be assessed. This will enable them to identify and gather evidence of progress throughout their school curriculum as well as activities and experiences outside school. Such an approach would also considerably ease the workload on teachers. Pupils will feel motivated to keep up and use their portfolios if it is clear to them that such an approach helps them to make progress and achieve.

Evaluation of citizenship education within the whole school

One purpose of assessment is to generate evidence of citizenship education by which a school can be held accountable. The role of inspection by OFSTED will, therefore, be important in recognising achievements in citizenship and in evaluating whole-school ethos, particularly in relation to citizenship. From 2002 OFSTED will be obliged to inspect for citizenship provision as a separate subject within secondary schools. In addition, the government green paper *Schools, Building on Success* (DfEE 2001) sees citizenship as having a vital contribution to make to what it calls 'education with character' – education that aims to impart not only knowledge and understanding but also to develop skills, attitudes and 'habits of mind'. These habits of mind include entrepreneurship, motivation, teamwork, creativity and flexibility. The paper stresses the need for schools to focus on the contribution of whole-school ethos to the development of 'education with character' and, in particular, the need to involve pupils more actively within schools. School councils are specifically mentioned – the important point here being that for such councils to be successful, they must have real power. The paper stresses the need for schools to think precisely about the contribution they make to the community and how to make community partnerships work more effectively for everyone. The evaluation of whole-school provision for citizenship will also need to be considered, therefore, by governors and schools.

The success of citizenship education as a live, challenging and fundamental aspect of whole-school culture and ethos will depend in part, therefore, on how OFSTED choose to frame their inspection. OFSTED inspection of citizenship within the whole school could be another way to raise the status of this area. The need to include wider, whole-school and participatory achievements will be important if citizenship is really seen to make a vital contribution to the education of each pupil. Evidence of whole-school achievement in citizenship could be used as an additional qualitative indicator on 'school performance tables'.

Qualifications and certificates in citizenship

Why certificate progress and achievement in citizenship?

Traditionally, it has been argued that qualifications ensure that pupil achievements are valued, helping to motivate pupils, giving status and making assessment more rigorous and consistent. These assumptions, however, will need to be carefully examined in the light of the particular needs and nature of citizenship education and weighed up against the possible negative impact of a less holistic, more formal and standardised assessment on the nature of teaching and learning in citizenship. In addition, qualifications have been seen as a useful means of making schools accountable for the education they provide. There are alternative methods of providing evidence for purposes of accountability, such as inspection and school evaluation, which may not have a negative impact on curriculum provision.

The question of accrediting achievement and progression in citizenship at Key Stage 4 and beyond is a problematic one. Such a system of certification will need to satisfy a number of principles. It will need to provide progression from Key Stage 3 and to post-16 while recognising that provision at Key Stages 3 and 4 is likely to be varied and diverse. It will need to be inclusive of *all* pupils, motivating them, meeting their needs and interests and having a real relevance and meaning to their lives. It will need to reflect the programme of study at Key Stage 4 while, at the same time, recognising the breadth and flexibility of the programme of study, which enables schools to provide for citizenship in a variety of ways. It will need to allow the achievements of *all* pupils to be recognised and offer opportunities for all to reflect on their progress. It will need to assess participation and active involvement of pupils if it is to be a valid assessment of citizenship.

The challenge of assessing the participatory aspects of citizenship, in particular, within a qualification should not be underestimated. Comparability within qualifications tends to be achieved by ensuring that assessment tasks are presented in the same way to all pupils, assessment criteria are interpreted in the same way by all teachers and performance is judged in the same way by all assessors.

Since it is unlikely that one qualification could satisfy all the requirements outlined above, there will be need for a suite of awards if citizenship education or some aspects of it, are to be assessed for the purpose of certificating pupil achievement. In addition, further work will need to be done to investigate using models of assessment that provide a valid and dependable assessment of an area such as citizenship.

Given the challenges involved in certificating achievement in citizenship, it will be important for schools and teachers to think carefully whether providing opportunities for pupils to gain qualifications in citizenship is suitable for their citizenship provision. Many schools may choose not to go down the qualification route because there is nothing on offer that would enhance their citizenship curriculum and much that could distort and narrow whole-school provision. This does not mean that schools will not be assessing citizenship, simply that they will not be offering qualifications or following a specification. Other schools may welcome the structure that a specification provides as well as the opportunity to recognise pupil achievement with an external award.

Possible approaches

At present, although there are qualifications which assess some aspects of citizenship education, there is no qualification on offer which reflects the statutory programme of study in citizenship for Key Stage 4. Types of qualifications which are relevant for Key Stage 4 (levels 1 and 2 of the national qualification framework) include: GNVQ (foundation and intermediate), GCSE, Entry Level (below GCSE and broadly equivalent to National Curriculum levels 1 to 3). There are also relevant awards such as those for community service, including the Duke of Edinburgh awards.

There are problems with recognising achievement in citizenship education, or aspects of it, within the existing qualifications. Appropriate GCSEs are not all necessarily compulsory – all pupils will not sit all of them and titles do not include the word 'citizenship'. If the decision were taken to distinguish citizenship 'units' within existing types of qualifications, banking them and providing separate certification, changes would have to be made to modularise relevant GCSEs and provide for unitised certification. Entry-level qualifications would need to be developed to ensure that all pupils have access to certification of achievement in citizenship. GNVQ would also need some adaptations but current GNVQ provision is intended to remain unchanged until 2004. Teaching and assessment programmes would need to be devised that ensured balanced and coherent coverage of the programme of study in citizenship for Key Stage 4.

One possible approach is the introduction of a Short Course GCSE in Citizenship Studies, made possible by the development of subject specific criteria by the QCA. The choice of title is significant and sends a clear message that this is not assessment of citizenship but of a particular and partial aspect of it. The choice of title is also intended to avoid the idea that pupils can 'fail' as citizens. Is this an adequate solution or does it run the risk of confusing the two? 'Citizenship Studies' is not a qualification in 'citizenship' but a separate area of learning. It will be important to keep the distinction in mind while, at the same time, exploring and understanding how citizenship education and Citizenship Studies can relate to each other.

This approach is similar to that already taken for physical education, where there is a statutory obligation to provide for programmes of study within the curriculum plus an option to take a qualification if it is advantageous to do so. Many schools currently provide an extra lesson for those taking a qualification in PE as well as covering the programme of study.

If the distinction between Citizenship Studies GCSE and citizenship education is not well understood, the impact of a qualification could be a negative one. Citizenship could become a much narrower experience than the programme of study intends, rewarding knowledge and understanding at the expense of participation and process. Furthermore the whole-school, community-based aspects of citizenship could be neglected as well as the requirement to develop knowledge and understanding through the development of particular skills. Care will need to be taken that citizenship teaching and learning does not become discrete, less innovative, less flexible and whole school than it is intended to be or required to be.

Given the possible impact of GCSE assessment on teaching and learning styles in citizenship, the nature of the subject criteria are very important as will be the models submitted by the awarding bodies in response. The criteria allow for up to 40 per cent internal assessment or course work while at least 60 per cent must be assessed externally. Forty per cent internal assessment is higher than the 25 per cent limit for other GCSEs and reflects the need for internal assessment methods to recognise progression and achievement in the participatory aspects of the citizenship programme of study at Key Stage 4. Is 40 per cent adequate to cover both parts 2 and 3 of the programme of study? In addition, how will the separate assessment of knowledge and skills, part 1, from skills, impact on teaching and learning styles? What issues will be raised by assessing parts 2 and 3 internally? Teachers may need to work with other assessors within the school and wider community, designing learning experiences, objectives and assessment outcomes. Assessment opportunities will need to be varied, including observation and self-assessment as well as questioning, written work and oral work. Moderation will need to take place to enhance consistency of judgements reached and support higher quality assessments by teachers and others. Many teachers may be concerned about the increased workload of a GCSE with 40 per cent internal assessment.

In addition, the current credibility and status of course work or internal assessment is not high. While course work would seem to be an ideal way to assess aspects of citizenship, it has been viewed with suspicion in England recently. Some suspicion relates to issues of equity and focuses on the possibility that some pupils may receive more and better help with their course work from their parents (Gipps 1994). In citizenship, however, the point has already been made that getting help to make progress is part of the learning process. Very clear guidelines will need to be laid down, therefore, for internal assessment of citizenship and it may be desirable to develop a model that rewards individual progress and mastery in metacognitive skills and aptitudes rather than outcomes as compared with others. Short Course GCSE will need to be the first small step in development of qualifications for citizenship. A broader range of qualifications, including Entry Level will also need to be developed to give *all* pupils access at Key Stage 4.

The Creativity, Action and Service component of the International Baccalaureate examination might be a useful model when thinking about the place of citizenship assessment within qualifications. The Creativity, Action and Service is a central feature of the International Baccalaureate curriculum. Its inclusion in the International Baccalaureate specification is intended to foster responsible and compassionate citizens. It requires participation in the community and, by doing so, develops in pupils greater awareness of themselves, concern for others and the ability to cooperate with others. This aspect of the International Baccalaureate is not, however, formally assessed. Instead informal self-evaluation by the student is encouraged – a process of reflecting on the benefits of participation and the understandings and skills acquired through participation. The decision not to assess Creativity, Action and Service is based on a concern that formal summative assessment for the purpose of certification and involving judgement of a standard is not appropriate for such an area of learning. The decision not to make the Creativity, Action and Service element into a high stakes part of the examination – affecting significantly grade outcomes for candidates – reflects an understanding of some of the consequences of high stakes assessments. High stakes assessments, as currently conceived, need rigorous processes of standardisation in order to enhance reliability and consistency of outcome. Assessments of citizenship education, however, cannot be easily standardised to ensure comparability between different assessors and the process of enhancing reliability involves changing the programme in ways that might make it less flexible and broad. One of the challenges for the International Baccalaureate is that it must operate in a wide range of contexts – including countries where community service can be life threatening; flexibility in a curriculum area such as Creativity, Action and Service is therefore vital.

Another possible approach is to use key skills for recognising achievement of aspects of citizenship education. Key skill units in Communication, Application of Number and Information Technology exist for pre-16 and post-16. There are also the 'wider' key skills of Working with Others, Problem Solving and Improving Own Learning and Performance, which have been developed but not yet approved as qualifications at any stage. These are highly relevant to citizenship education, focusing as they do on active, participatory and collaborative learning styles, where the learner is enabled and rewarded for taking responsibility for their own performance and progress. One of the problems in the development of these 'wider' key skills has been to find a context in which the skills that are considered 'key' can be practised. Citizenship education, as laid down by the programme of study, could be an appropriate context. Assessment of key skills is intended to be external and involve the use of portfolios – progress files that the pupil has ownership of and is required to manage. It is possible, therefore, that a productive relationship between these areas could ensue.

One problem with key skills, particularly the 'wider' three key skills, has been to ensure consistency of assessment. Finding innovative ways to assess participation, responsibility,

problem solving, skills of collaboration and communication are hampered by the preoc-
cupation with, in particular, the question of standardisation. It might be more productive,
therefore, to use self-assessment, bench marking – focusing on valid ways to recognise
achievement and progression of an individual, without reference to levels of attainment
or comparisons with others. If the purpose of the assessment is to improve and recognise individual progress and achievement then there is no need for a system that makes
comparisons.

Another possible way forward is the use of awards in citizenship that could depend
upon the active participation of the pupil and, ideally, the community. Assessment would
need to be formative and criterion referenced to ensure flexibility of approach within
different communities and cultures. Quality standards could ensure that young people are
entitled to a high quality and distinctive learning experience by specifying clearly the
opportunities that must be built in to the award programme. For example, 'if a person
does this award they are entitled to: have opportunities to reflect on progress, opportunities to progress as member of a team; opportunities to take the lead, and so on.

Conclusion

The success and quality of assessment in citizenship education will depend primarily upon
how schools, and others with influence, view the purposes of assessment in citizenship
and the degree to which they are able to select and use appropriate and effective assessment models which are fit for these purposes. The main purpose of assessment in citizenship education must be to improve learning and enable progress to take place.
Progress in citizenship must involve developing metacognitive skills and dispositions as
well as knowledge and understanding. Finding ways to give feedback that is effective in
developing these skills and dispositions is, therefore, a major challenge of citizenship
assessment. Schools, teachers and pupils will need resources and guidance, including
support for moderation procedures, if they are to meet the challenge effectively. If qualifications in citizenship education or aspects of it are to be offered to schools, a political
will must exist for investigating new models of assessment that can accredit progression
and achievement within the particular nature of citizenship education.

Tasks

TASK 8. 1

Challenges of citizenship assessment

In groups, brainstorm in what ways citizenship assessment will be challenging for schools, teachers and pupils.

Prioritise three challenges as being the most important. Why did you make these choices?

Discuss possible approaches and solutions to each of the three challenges.

Note: While you were working as a group to share ideas, make choices and reach conclusions, you were practising skills of citizenship. How could your performance be assessed? What assessment outcomes could have been looked for? What assessment methods could have been used? What challenges might assessing your performance both as a team and as individual team members pose?

TASK 8. 2

Thinking about the purpose of assessment

Discuss the reasons given above for assessing progression and achievement in citizenship education.

Are they all valid? Do you agree with all of the reasons given? Do you disagree with some?

Prioritise the three most important reasons for assessing citizenship. Compare your choices with others. Discuss the similarities and the difference between your choices.

Did you think that any other purposes, not mentioned above, are relevant and important?

Does everyone agree that it is necessary to assess citizenship?
Why/why not?

TASK 8. 3

Learning objectives for pupils

How could the following 'teacher' learning objectives be presented to pupils in a Year 7 class so that they are meaningful to all?

Learning objectives
(i) know about the diversity of ethnic identities within the United Kingdom.
(ii) recognise the importance of mutual respect and understanding.

You may also want to consider how further relevant and meaningful objectives could be negotiated between teacher and pupils.

In what circumstances might some pupils need individual learning objectives?

TASK. 8. 4

Progression in citizenship education

Imagine a discussion about a controversial moral, social or political issue, for example, euthanasia, abortion, abolition of Lords, capital punishment, freedom of speech, freedom of information. If a second discussion of a similar type was planned to follow up the first discussion, how could progression between the two occur?

Below are set out the assessment criteria (what are we – the assessors– looking for?) for discussion No.1.

Assessment criteria
(i) pupil listens to others and responds to their views;
(ii) pupils show respect for differences of opinion; and
(iii) pupils use their knowledge and understanding of issues during discussion.

What assessment criteria would you set for a series of discussions on it? How would pupils demonstrate progress?

TASK 8. 5

Supporting reflection and self-assessment

To help pupils to self-assess their work both during the process of producing it and after:

Design a list of key questions to be displayed in the classroom for all pupils across Key Stage 3 to use at all times.

For example,
What are you finding difficult?
Has anyone or anything helped you to understand something or do something new? How did they do this?

Add at least four more key assessment questions to the list.
What other ideas do you have about supporting pupil reflection and self-assessment during the production process?

TASK 8. 6

Planning for peer-assessment and self-assessment learning objectives

(i) to become more effective at self-assessment and peer-assessment; and
(ii) to work responsibly and effectively as a group member.

Set a task for small groups of pupils to complete as a team. For example, planning a debate, carrying out a content analysis of different newspapers to find out about the media, writing a manifesto for change and so on.

Design with pupils a 'self/peer-assessment sheet'. For example:

• participated in the group without being prompted;
• listened to what was being said and done;
• gave suggestions and ideas that helped the group achieve its task;
• made positive encouraging comments that helped the group;
• involved all the group by asking questions, allocating tasks; and
• spoke clearly, could be understood by all group members.

Each criterion could be given a 'rating', for example, 'yes' and 'no' or 'always', 'often', 'sometimes', 'rarely'.

At the end of the group activity, each pupil should complete a self-assessment sheet. These should then be circulated within each group.

Do peers agree or disagree with self-assessments?

In light of peer-assessments, pupils have opportunities to review and change their self-assessments.

How could the outcomes of this activity be used to support pupil progression in both:

- team work?
- Self-assessment and peer-assessment?

What ground rules would need be agreed to carry out the activity outlined above without putting at risk the self-esteem of individual pupils?

TASK. 8. 7

Progression and Values

A whole-class activity has been organised called 'Being British'. Pupils are given information about a wide variety of ethnic groups who have migrated to and settled in Britain, including Normans, Saxons, Jews, African Caribbean, Chinese, Kurdish and so on. Information given includes when and why they came to Britain and the contributions made to British culture. After discussing the information they are asked to reach a definition of 'what it means to be British'.

Assessment criteria
(i) pupil definition of 'what it means to be British' shows understanding that being British is not necessarily connected to language, religion, colour, customs and so on.

How can the teacher negotiate specific learning objectives with a pupil who holds racist beliefs and values that will enable them to participate in the activity and make progress in moral, social and political knowledge and understanding?

TASK 8. 8

Promoting participatory group review of progress during Key Stage

Learning objectives

(i) Pupils assess their own and others progress and achievements during the key stage.
(ii) Pupils work as a team to communicate and present their progress and achievements to the local community.

Select an activity that will enable pupils to achieve the above learning objectives, for example, assembly presentation, theatre piece, website, multimedia presentation, video, etc.

How could you, the teacher, use observation of the group processes and evidence from their presentation to assess their progress and achievements during the key stage?

What assessment criteria ('what I'm looking for') could you use?

TASK 8. 9

Supporting quality assessment from others, e.g. community partners

Design an interview schedule to be used by a community partner in order to support quality feedback.

You can either imagine that the feedback is to pupils planning a manifesto for change within the local community with community 'experts' such as councillors OR construct your own imaginary activity.

How could the questions be expressed in order that all assessors have focused and productive conversations with pupils about their progress and achievements in citizenship education?

TASK. 8.10

Assessing citizenship in a subject area

Learning objectives below are for a Year 9 history lesson on parliamentary reform.

- To know about the political system in Britain in 1815.
- To understand and use the term 'democratic', 'constituency', 'representation', Member of Parliament'.
- To know and understand why radicals wanted to change the system in 1815.

What learning objectives and assessment criteria could be included to develop understanding of aspects of the citizenship programme of study for Key Stage 3?

How could a physical education lesson where pupils play netball in two teams be used to develop and assess aspects of citizenship education? What learning objectives and assessment criteria could be included?

TASK 8.11

Using portfolios

You have been given responsibility within the school for producing guidance on portfolios for Year 7 pupils.

The portfolios will be kept until the end of Year 9 and used to help make judgements about progress and achievement in citizenship during Key Stage 3.

Make a list of what they will need to know and why.

What other strategies, apart from written guidance, could be used to support high-quality portfolios among your Year 7 pupils?

TASK 8.12

Impact of citizenship assessment on teaching and learning

Discuss how a GCSE in Citizenship Studies could impact on the nature of citizenship provision in schools at Key Stage 4.

In what ways might a GCSE in 'Political Studies' be appropriate for assessing aspects of citizenship?

In what ways might a GCSE in 'Political Studies' be inappropriate for assessing aspects of citizenship?

Conclusion

Every educational system has a moral goal that it tries to attain and that informs its curriculum. It wants to produce a certain kind of human being. This intention is more or less explicit, more or less a result of reflection; but even the neutral subjects, like reading and writing and arithmetic take their place in a vision of the educated person. In some nations the goal was the pious person, in others the warlike, in others the industrious. Always important is the political regime, which needs citizens who are in accord with its fundamental principle. Aristocracies want gentlemen, oligarchies men who respect and pursue money, and democracies lovers of equality. Democratic education, whether it admits it or not, wants and needs to produce men and women who have the tastes, knowledge, and character supportive of a democratic regime.

(Allan Bloom 1987: 26)

Teaching citizenship education in the secondary school should aim to ensure that pupils should not be the mere object of the learning process – they should be active and participatory learners. This means that the school, and its leadership at all levels, should also be participatory in governance. This will be a challenge to many schools that are not naturally democratic institution/communities. It is why citizenship education cannot be a new and partial form of education to be developed by itself, in isolation from the general school culture, curriculum and practice. It is, we have argued, a necessary dimension of the education process as a whole, and, as such, should be reflected in the taught curriculum – in all subjects and pastoral activities. It also plays a significant role in the selection of teaching strategies, the organisation of the school, the provision of extra-curricula activities, and for allowing the school community a real role in governing itself. Citizenship education begins with the ethos of the school. This is why it is essential that each school develop its own goals for citizenship education, which supports its own distinctive mission. In summary, we would conclude that citizenship education ought to be characterised by a number of general principles that seek actualisation within a school community. Among these are:

- ensuring that citizenship education is an integral part of the school's ethos, procedures and organisation;

- providing learning opportunities and experiences that are both meaningful and practical for the pupil;
- developing socially literate pupils;
- supporting pupils in seeing themselves as members of various structures: family, other groups, town, state, nation and international community, and to understand their rights and duties in each of these contexts;
- facilitating a sound understanding of pluralism and the diversity within society;
- offering opportunities for public policy investigations in the community in order that pupils can engage in participation;
- understanding that the political process of democracy is rooted in history as well as in contemporary applications;
- above all, making clear that citizenship education involves positive changes through the development of a pupil's dispositions, virtues, habits and general moral outlook.

In teaching citizenship education teachers will invariably adopt a multilevel perspective in which themes such as justice, tolerance and human rights will be considered at several levels – local, regional and global. Citizenship education is clearly not a subject that can be taught, as such, independently of the whole curriculum. Each school must ensure that there is a written policy on citizenship education as part of the school's development plan. It is therefore vital that the goals and purpose of citizenship education is clear and that the learning outcomes are also clearly stated in terms of what it is expected that pupils will know, understand and can do. However, we recognise that it is not always possible, or even desirable, to convert qualitative judgements into quantitative measures. In citizenship education it is not simply what pupils are taught that is important but what they actually learn through the experiences of school life itself. This is why the Citizenship Order could not usefully specify what a school should do in any detail for this depends on the general ethos and distinctive mission of the school as a particular community. What is essential for the teacher is that they recognise that each pupil needs a range of learning experiences to find their individual role in society. This is why Bentley concludes:

> So, learning to be a moral agent, and to be a citizen, begins in the family and the school. But surely citizenship extends beyond these institutions? The goal of citizenship education is to enable young people to develop into active responsible citizens in the wider world. Schools are the institutions which contain a young person's activity for most of their first two decades, but they also live in the wider world; they are members of numerous communities, more diverse than school-based learning opportunities, however good these might be. As young people grow into the wider world, it is appropriate to seek opportunities to extend their problem-solving abilities, their concern for others, and their exercise of ethical conduct beyond the school gates.
>
> (Bentley 1988: 66)

We believe this accurately summarises much of what we have argued for and discussed in this introductory text. Citizenship education requires a fresh approach in schools.

References and further reading

Annette, J. (2000) 'Education for citizenship: civic participation and experiential and service learning in the community', in Lawton, D. Cairns, J. and Gardner, R. (eds) *Education for Citizenship*. London: Continuum

Arthur, J. (1999a) 'Communitarianism: what are the implications for education', *Educational Studies* **24** (3), 353–68.

Arthur, J. (1999b) *Schools and Community: The Communitarian Agenda in Education*. London: Falmer Press.

Arthur, J. and Davison, J. (2000) 'Social literacy and citizenship education in the school curriculum', *The Curriculum Journal* **11** (1), 9–23.

Arthur, J., Davison, J. and Stow, W. (2000) *Social Literacy, Citizenship and the National Curriculum*. London: Falmer Press.

Arthur, J., Davis, I., Hadyn, T., Kerr, D. and Wrenn, A. (2001) *Citizenship and the Teaching of History*. London: Routledge/Falmer Press.

Bailey, R. (ed.) (2000) *Teaching Values and Citizenship Across the Curriculum*. London: Kogan Page.

Banham, D. and Dawson, I. (2000) *This is History – King John*. London: John Murray.

Batho, G. (1990) 'The history of the teaching of civics and citizenship in English schools', *The Curriculum Journal* **1** (1), 91–100.

Beck, J. (1998) *Morality and Citizenship in Education*. London: Cassell.

Bell, D. (1993) *Communitarianism and its Critics*. Oxford: Clarendon Press.

Bellah, R. N., Madsen, R., Sullivan, W. M., Swidler, A. and Tipton, S. M. (1985) *Habits of the Heart: Individualism and Commitment in American Life*. Berkley: University of California Press.

Bentley, T. (1998) *Learning Beyond the Classroom*. London: Demos/Routledege.

Black, P. and Wiliam, D. (1998) 'Assessment and classroom learning', *Assessment in Education* **5** (1), 7–74.

Bloom, A. (1987) *The Closing of the American Mind*. London: Penguin.

Bousted, M. and Davies, I. (1996) 'Teachers' perceptions of models of political learning', *Curriculum* **17** (1), 12–23.

Broadfoot, P., Osborne, M., Planel, C. and Sharpe, K. (2000) *Promoting Quality in Learning: Does England have the Answer?* London: Cassell.

Callan, E. (1997) *Creating Citizens: Political Education in a Liberal Democracy*. Oxford: Oxford University Press.

Carr, D. and Steutel, J. (1999) *Virtue Ethics and Moral Education*. London: Routledge.

Children's Society (1991) *Education for Citizenship: A resource pack for Key Stage 3*. London: The Children's Society.

Citizenship Foundation (1994) *The Importance of Citizenship*, evidence submitted to the National Commission on Education, Insights into Education and Training. London: Heinneman.

Citizenship Foundation (1995) *Can They Do That: Learning About Active Citizenship*. London: Citizenship Foundation.

Colley, L. (1994) *Britons: Forging the Nation 1707–1837*. London: Pimlico.

Community Service Volunteers (2000) *Discovering Citizenship Through Active Learning in the Community: A Teaching Toolkit*. London: CSV.

Conrad, D. and Hedin, D. (1991) 'School-based community service: what we know from research and theory', *Phi Delta Kappan* **72**: 745–57.

Crewe, I., Sewing, D. and Conover, (1997) *Citizenship and Civic Education*. London: Citizenship Foundation.

Crick, B. (2000) *Essays on Citizenship*. London: Continuum.

Crick, B. and Lister, I. (1978) 'Political literacy', in Crick, B. and Porter, A. (eds) *Political Education and Political Literacy*. London: Longman.

Crick, B. and Porter, A. (eds) (1990) *Political Education and Political Literacy*. London: Longman.

Crooks, T. J. (1998) 'The impact of classroom evaluation practices on students', *Review of Educational Research*, **58** (4), 438–81.

Davies, I. (1994) 'Whatever happened to political literacy?', *Educational Review* **46** (1), 15–27.

Davies, I. (1995) 'Education for European citizenship and the teaching and learning of history', in Osler, A., Rathenow, H.-F. and Starkey, H. (eds) *Teaching for Citizenship in Europe*. Stoke on Trent: Trentham Books.

Davies, I. (1999) 'What has happened in the teaching of politics in schools in England in the last three decades and why?', *Oxford Review of Education* **25** (1) and (2), 125–40.

Davies, I., Gray, G. and Stephens, P. (1998) 'Education for Citizenship: a case study of "Democracy Day" at a comprehensive school', *Educational Review* **50** (1), 15–27.

Davies, I., Gregory, I. and Riley, S. C. (1999) *Good Citizenship and Educational Provision*. London: Falmer Press.

Deem, R., Brehony, K. and Heath, S. (1995) *Active Citizenship and the Governing of School*. Buckingham: Open University Press.

Department for Education and Employment (2001) *Schools: Building on Success*. London: Stationary Office.

Department for Education and Employment/Qualifications and Curriculum Authority (1999) *Citizenship. The National Curriculum for England*. London: DfEE/QCA.

Department for Education and Employment/Qualifications and Curriculum Authority (1999a) *Citizenship: Key Stages 3–4*. London: DfEE/QCA.

Department for Education and Employment/Qualifications and Curriculum Authority (1999b) *Framework for Personal Social and Health Education and Citizenship at Key Stages 1 and 2*. London: DfEE/QCA.

Department for Education and Employment (2000) *Remembering Genocides: Lessons for the Future*. London: DfEE.

Desforges, C. (ed.) (1995) *An Introduction to Teaching*. Oxford: Blackwell.

Dewey, J. (1926) *Democracy and Education*. New York: Macmillan.

Doyal, L. and Gough, I. (1991) *Theory of Human Need*. Basingstoke: Macmillan.

Dyson, A. and Robson, E. (1999) *School, Family and Community*. London: Roundtree Foundation.

Eisner, E. W. (1993) 'Reshaping Assessment in Education: Some criteria in search of practice', *Journal of Curriculum Studies* **25** (3), 219–33.

Enslin, P. (2000) 'Education and Democratic Citizenship, in Leicester', M., Modgil, C. and Modgil, S. (eds) *Politics, Education and Citizenship*. London: Falmer Press.

Etzioni, A. (1995) *The Spirit of Community*. New York: Basic Books.

Etzioni, A. (1997) *The New Golden Rule: community and morality in a democratic society*. New York: Basic Books.

Foster, J. (ed.) (2000) *Citizenship in Focus* series. London: HarperCollins.

Further Education Funding Council (2001) *Report of the Advisory Group for Citizenship 16–19 Year Olds*. London.

Garratt, D. (2000) 'Democratic citizenship in the curriculum: some problems and possibilities', *Pedagogy, Culture and Society* **8** (3), 322–46.

Giddens, A. (1998) *The Third Way: The Renewal of Social Democracy*. London: Polity Press.

Gipps, C. and Stobart, G. (1993) *Assessment: A Teachers' Guide to the Issues*. London: Hodder & Stoughton.

Gipps, C. V. (1994) *Beyond Testing: Towards a Theory of Educational Assessment*. London: Falmer Press.

Gilbert, R. (1996) 'What are the people?: education, citizenship and the Civics Expert Group Report', *Curriculum Perspectives* **16** (1), 56–61.

Goldby, M. (1997) 'Communitarianism and Education', *Curriculum Studies* **5** (2), 125–38.

Griffith, R. (1998) *Educational Citizenship and Independent Learning*. London: Jessica Kingsley Publishers.

Hadyn, T., Arthur, J. and Hunt, M. (1997) *Learning to Teach History in the Secondary School*. London: Routledge.

Halstead, J. M. and McLaughlin, T. H. (eds) (1999) *Education and Morality*. London: Routledge.

Hampshire County Council (2000) *Citizenship Education Planning Framework*. Hampshire County Council.

Hart, R. (1992) *Children's Participation: From Tokenism to Citizenship*, Innocenti Essays No. 4, Florence, UNICEF International Child Development Centre.

Heater, D. (1990) *Citizenship: The Civic Ideal in World History, Politics and Education*. London: Longman.

Heater, D. (1999) *What is Citizenship?* Cambridge: Polity Press.

Held, D. (1995) *Democracy and the Global Order: From the Modern State to Cosmopolitan Governance*. Cambridge: Polity Press.

Hill, B., Pike, G. and Selby, D. (1998) *Perspectives on Childhood: An Approach to Citizenship Education*. London: Cassell.

Holden, C. and Clough, N. (eds) (2000) *Children as Citizens: Education for Participation*. London: Jessica Kingsley.

Hughes, S. (2000) 'Subject leadership: resource management', in Field, K. (ed.) *Subject Leadership*. London: The Stationary Office, 389–449.

Ichilov, O. (ed.) (1998) *Citizenship and Citizenship Education in a Changing World*. London: Woburn Press.

Institute for Citizenship (2000) *Citizenship Update*. Autumn edition, London.

Kennedy, K. J. (ed.) (1997) *Citizenship Education and the Modern State*. London: Falmer Press.

Kerr, D. (1999) *Re-examining Citizenship Education: The Case of England*. Slough: NFER.

Kymlicka, W. (1999) 'Education for Citizenship', in Halstead, J. M. and McLaughlin, T. H. (eds) *Education and Morality*. London: Routledge.

Lawton, D., Cairns, J. and Gardner, R. (eds) (2000a) *Education for Citizenship*. London: Continuum.

Lawton, D. Cairns, J. and Gardner, R. (eds) (2000b) *Education for Values: Morals, Ethics and Citizenship in Contemporary Teaching*. London: Kogan Page.

Leddington, D. and Tudor, R. (forthcoming) *Practical Resources for the Teaching of Citizenship in the Secondary School*. London: David Fulton Publishers.

Leicester, M., Modgil, C. and Modgil, S. (eds) (2000) *Politics, Education and Citizenship*. London: Falmer Press.

Lloyd, J. (2000) *'Success for Everyone': Benchmarks for Citizenship*. City of Birmingham: Birmingham Health Education.

Lloyd-Jones, R. ([1985] 1995) *How to Produce Better Worksheets*. London: Stanley Thornes.

Lynch, J. (1992) *Education for Citizenship in a Multi-Cultural Society*. London: Cassell.

McCallum B. (2000) *Formative Assessment – Implications for Classroom Practice*, London, Institute of Education.

McIntyre, A. (1999) 'How to seem virtuous without actually being so', in Halstead, J. M. and McLaughlin, T. H. (eds) *Education and Morality*. London: Routledge.

McLaughlin, T. H. (2000) 'Citizenship education in England: the Crick Report and beyond', *Journal of Philosophy of Education* **34** (4), 541–70.

McLaughlin, T. H. (1992) 'Citizenship, diversity and education: a philosophical perspective', *Journal of Moral Education* **21** (3), 235–50.

Marshall, T. H. (1963) *Sociology at the Crossroads and Other Essays*. London: Heinemann.

Marshall, T. H. (1963) 'Citizenship and Social Class', in Marshall, T. H.(ed.) *Sociology at the Crossroads and Other Essays*. London: Heinemann.

Marton F. and Booth S. (1997) *Learning and Awareness*. Mahwah, NJ: Lawrence Erlbaum.

Morris, L. (1994) *Dangerous Classes: The Underclass and Social Citizenship*. London: Routledge.

National Curriculum Council (1990) *Education for Citizenship* (Curriculum Guidance 8). York: NCC.

National Forum for Values in Education and the Community (1996) *Values in Education and the Community: Final Report and Recommendations*. London: SCAA.

Phillips, R. (1998b) 'Contesting the past, constructing the future: politics, policy and identity in schools', *British Journal of Educational Studies* **1** (46), 40–53.

Popenoe, D. (1994) 'The roots of declining social virtues: family, community and the need for a "Natural Communities Policy"', in Popenoe, D., Norton, A. and Maley, B.(eds) *Shaping Social Virtues*. St. Leonards: NSW, Australia, Centre for Independent Studies.

Potter, J. (1999) *The Why and How of Citizenship Education: The Case for Active Learning in the Community*. London: CVS.

Qualifications and Curriculum Authority (1998a) *Education for Citizenship and the Teaching of Democracy in Schools*. QCA: London.

Qualifications and Curriculum Authority (1998b) *Developing the School Curriculum.* Sudbury: QCA.

Qualifications and Curriculum Authority (1999a*) History: The National Curriculum for England.* QCA: London.

Qualifications and Curriculum Authority (1999b*) Rationale for the School Curriculum and Functions of the National Curriculum.* QCA: London.

Qualifications and Curriculum Authority (2000) *Citizenship at Key Stage 3 and 4 Initial Guidance for Schools.* QCA: London.

Qualifications and Curriculum Authority/Department for Education and Employment (2000) *Personal Social and Health Education and Citizenship at Key Stages 1 and 2: Initial Guidance for Schools.* London: QCA/DfEE.

Rowe, D. (2000) 'Values, pluralism, democracy and education for citizenship', in Leicester, M., Modgil, C. and Modgil, S. (eds) *Politics, Education and Citizenship.* London: Falmer Press.

Ruddock, J. and Flutter, J. (2000) 'Pupil participation and the pupil perspective: carving a new order of experience', *Cambridge Journal of Education* **30** (1), 75–89.

Runnymede Trust (2000) *Commission on the Future of Multi-Ethnic Britain.* London: Runnymede Trust.

Sadler, D. R. (1989) 'Formative assessment and the design of instructional systems', *Instructional Science* **18**, 119–44.

Saunders, L. (1995) *Education for Life.* Slough: NFER.

Simon, R. (1999) 'For a pedagogy of possibility', in Pierce, B. 'Towards a pedagogy of possibility in the teaching of English internationally: people's English in South Africa', *TESOL Quarterly* **23** (3), 401–20.

South Africa (2000) *Values Education and Democracy – Report of the Working Group on Values in Education.* South Africa: Ministry of Education.

Speaker's Commission (1990) *Encouraging Citizenship.* London: HMSO.

Stenhouse, L. (1970) *The Humanities Curriculum Project.* London: Heinemann.

Stradling, R., Noctor, M. and Baines, B. (1984) *Teaching Controversial Issues.* London: Edward Arnold.

Teacher Training Agency (2000, unpublished) 'The Twelve Consultancy – Citizenship NQT Demand', Telephone Research (July 2000). London: TTA.

Tooley, J. (2000) *Reclaiming Education.* London: Cassell.

Trafford, B. (1997) *Participation, Power Sharing and School Improvement in UK Education.* Nottingham: Heretics Press.

UNICEF (2000) *Citizenship in Schools – A Baseline Survey of Curriculum and Practice.* London: United Nations Children's Fund.

UNICEF (2001) *Citizenship in 400 Schools.* London: United Nations Children's Fund.

Watkins, C., Carnell, E., Lodge, C. and Whalley, C. (1996) *Effective Learning. School Improvement Network Bulletin Research Matters.* London: Institute of Education.

Wellington, J. J. (1986) *Controversial Issues in the Curriculum.* Oxford: Blackwell.

White, J. (1990) *Education and the Good Life: Beyond the National Curriculum.* London: Kogan Page.

Voiels, V. (1998) 'New teachers talking citizenship', in Holden, C. and Clough, N. (eds) *Children as Citizens: Education for Participation.* London: Jessica Kingsley.

Young, M. (1999) 'Knowledge, learning and the curriculum of the future', *British Educational Research Journal,* 463–77.

www.qca.org.uk/ca/5-14/afl

Index

Absolutely No Limits 110
abstract ideas, teaching of 73
academicising 40, 44
accountability 50, 52
accreditation of citizenship education 41, 50, 53–5, 128
Advisory Group on Education for Citizenship and the Teaching of Democracy 9, 30
advocacy 88
affective domain, teaching of 77–8
analogy, teaching by 74-5
Annette, J. 87
art 25
Arthur, J. 86, 115
assemblies 112
assessment
    citizenship education 50–5, 123–44
        evaluation within whole school 127, 133–4
        formative assessment 129, 130–1
        main issues in 126–9
        national requirements and developments 124-5
        OFSTED inspection 125, 133
        qualifications and certificates 126, 134-8
        reasons for assessment 129
        recording and reporting 132–3
        summative assessment 129, 131-2
        tasks 139–44
    experiential learning 96–7
Association of Citizenship Teachers 66
Association for Education in Citizenship 6
audit 46
authoritarianism 72
autonomy of the child 72

Barclays New Futures 62, 63, 110
Bentley, T. 146
bias 76–7, 78–80, 103
Birmingham Education Authority 94-5
Bloom, Allan 145
Brehony, K. 35

British Council 66
British Nationality Act 1981 6
Broadfoot, P. 7
business and vocational education 25-6

Carr, D. 13
case study of implementation of citizenship education 38–53
Centre for Citizenship Studies in Education 57–8
certificates 126, 134-8
change
    forces of 32
    management of 49
Charter 88 112
Children's Express 116
Children's Society 107
Citizen and the Law textbook 108
Citizenship for All 108
Citizenship Consultation Group 58
citizenship education 10–11, 20–37, 46, 101, 145-6
    argument for 40–2
    concepts in 31-2
    coordinator for 23
    definitions 4-19
        community involvement 9–10, 12, 13–14
        political literacy 10, 12, 14
        social and moral responsibility 9, 12–13
    dispositions 32–3
    as distinct subject 30–1
    experiences 33
    in Scotland 14-16
    theoretical background 6–11
    whole school and 22, 33–5, 36, 43
        assessment 127, 133–4
    see also individual topics
Citizenship in Focus series 110–11
Citizenship Foundation 4, 7, 58–60, 105, 107, 108, 112
Citizenship Order 1-3, 11-14, 30, 40, 42, 72, 77, 146

Clough, N. 88
Coalition for Citizenship 7, 56, 57, 103, 105
Colley, Linda 17
Commission on Citizenship 7
communitarianism 86–7
communities
    definition 88
    identification of needs of 88
    implementation of 'solutions' 88
    involvement in 9–10, 12, 13–14
        resources for 109–10
        see also experiential learning in the community
    school as community 39
    social systems and structures 31
Community Service Volunteers (CSV) 7, 62–4, 86,
    88, 92–3, 99, 109
conflict
    in groups 91
    nature and sources of 32
conformism 40
controversial ideas, teaching of 75-6, 103
coordinator for citizenship education 23
Costello, P. J. M. 84
Council for Citizenship and Learning in the
    Community (CCLC) 62
Council for Education in World Citizenship 7, 64-
    5, 106
Council for Environmental Education 66
Council of Europe 58
craft, design and technology 26
creation of own resources 113–15
Crick, Bernard 1, 9, 10, 14, 15, 18, 20, 41, 48, 58,
    59, 68, 76, 126
critical faculties, development of 80–1
curriculum *see* National Curriculum

Davies, I. 5, 22, 34, 43, 73
decision making 31
deductive reasoning 74
Deem, R. 35
Democracy in Action 110
Democracy Days 34, 43
design and technology 26
Dewey, John 56
differentiation of resources 115-16
direct action 88
Directory of Community Organisations 66
Discovering Citizenship 62, 63, 109–10
discussion 75-6
dispositions 32–3
Doyal, L. 90
drama 26
duties and rights 74
Dyson, A. 85

Economic and Social Research Council 58
Education Act 1996 54, 82

Education for Citizenship resource pack 107
Education Reform Act 1988 10, 92
Eisner, E. W. 96–7
Election Pack 66
elections 31
    school/mock 34, 43, 66, 111
English 26, 29, 30, 43
Enslin, Penny 8
Etzioni, A. 86–7
European Convention on Human Rights 108
European Parliament 113
European Union 113
exclusion 8
experiences 33
experiential learning in the community 85-100
    assessment 96–7
    group work strategies 91-3
    methods 96
    planning 93–6

Fairfield High School 105
families, planning community participation and 93
Flutter, J. 87
foreign languages 28
formative assessment 129, 130–1
Foster, J. 110
France, notion of citizenship in 6–7

Garratt, D. 12, 87
GCSE in Citizenship Studies 126, 128, 135-6
geography 27, 29, 30
Gilbert, R. 6
Gipps, C. V. 136
Global Concerns 110–11
GNVQ 135
Good Thinking 108
Gough, I. 90
government 31
Gregory, I. 5
Griffith, r. 71
group work 90-3
Guardian 116

Hadyn, T. 115
Hampshire Education Authority 94, 100
Hampshire Grid for Learning 104, 115
Hansard Society 7, 65-6, 111-12
Hart, R. 88
Health Schools project 64
Heater, Derek 7
Heath, S. 35
history 27, 29, 30, 76
Holden, C. 89
Holocaust Memorial Day 108–9
Houses of Parliament 111, 112
Hughes, S. 113
Human Rights ImpACT 107–8

Human Rights textbook 108
Humanities Curriculum Project 72
Hunt, M. 115

identification of needs 88
impartiality 72
indirect action 88
indoctrination 72, 76–7
information, communication and technology (ICT) 27, 43
Institute for Citizenship 7, 61, 105, 106
integrationalism 48
International Baccalaureate 136–7
Introducing Citizenship distance learning package 60
Islington Arts and Media School 105

Jones, Bernard 76–7

Kellner, Peter 72
Kerr, D. 6
key skills approach 137–8
Kymlicka, Wil 2

Labour Party (New Labour), citizenship education and 2, 10, 12, 24
language
    foreign languages 28
    use of 114
learning *see* experiential learning in the community; teaching and learning in citizenship
Learning for Citizenship distance learning course 57
Learning and Skills Development Agency 68–9
Leddington, D. 101
Lighthouse Schools 62, 63
Lister, I. 14
literacy 43, 62
    political *see* political literacy
Lloyd, J. 95
Lloyd-Jones, R. 115

McCallum, B. 131
McIntyre, A. 98
McLaughlin, T. H. 12, 88
management of change 49
Marshall, T. H. 9
mathematics 28, 43
mock elections 34, 43, 66, 111
Mock Trial Competitions 60
Model United Nations 64
moderation 51, 132
modular structures 35
monarchy 112
Moral Education in Secondary Schools Project 59
moral responsibility 9, 12–13
    resources for 107–9
Morris, L. 8
motivation 41
Munn, Pamela 15

music 28

National Curriculum 10–11, 20–37, 71
    citizenship education and 10–11, 20–37, 46, 101
        assessment 124-5
        Citizenship Order 1-3, 11-14, 30, 40, 42, 72, 77, 146
        concepts in 31-2
        dispositions 32–3
        as distinct subject 30–1
        experiences 33
        planning 21-4
        subject curriculum and 24-31
        whole school and 22, 33–5, 36, 43, 127, 133–4
    National Curriculum Council 7
National Forum of Values in Education and the Community 24, 45
National Foundation for Education Research (NFER) 106
National Grid for Learning 103, 104
National Year of Reading (NYR) 62
needs, identification of 88
Negotiated Learning 64
Nelson Thornes 106
neutrality 72, 81
New Futures 62, 63, 110
New Labour *see* Labour Party (New Labour)
newspapers 115-16
Northern Ireland 58, 112
numeracy 43

objectivity 81
Office for Standards in Education (OFSTED) 93, 125, 133
organisations 56–69
    guidance on resources 103–4
Ousedale School case study 38–53

Parliament 111, 112
Passport for Life 110
Pearson Publishing 105, 107
pedagogy 81
peer mentoring 64
Pennywell School 64
personal, social and moral education (PSE) 28, 44
physical education 28–9
planning
    approaches to citizenship education 21-4
    community participation 93–6
    formative assessment 130–1
    summative assessment 131-2
political literacy 10, 12, 14
    resources for 110–13
political system 31
Porter, A. 14
portfolios 51
Potter, John 86, 93

power 32
presentation 114
Prime Minister 112
progress files 51
projects and organisations 56–69
propaganda 44-5

qualifications and certificates 126, 134-8
Qualifications and Curriculum Authority (QCA)
    68, 70, 82, 93, 103, 104, 125, 126
qualitative issues 49

re-conceptualisation 49
record keeping 52–3, 132–3
regional and local partnerships 64
relevancy 56
religious education 29
Remembering Genocides 109
reporting 52–3, 132–3
resistance 45
resources 101-22
    creation of own resources 113–15
    differentiation 115-16
    key strands and 104-7
        community involvement 109–10
        political literacy 110–13
        social and moral responsibility 107–9
    organisations providing guidance on 103–4
    tasks 116–22
rights and duties 74
Riley, S. C. 5
Robson, E. 85
Roehampton Institute 63
Rosemary School 105
Rowe, Don 7–8
Ruddock, J. 87
Runnymede Trust 17, 109

Sadler, D. R. 129
schools
    case study of implementation of citizenship
        education 38–53
    as communities 39
    ethos 33–4
    participation in community projects 85-100
    whole school and citizenship education 22,
        33–5, 36, 43
        assessment 127, 133–4
    see also National Curriculum
Schools Council UK 65-6, 109
science 29
Scotland
    citizenship education in 14-16
    Scottish Parliament 112
self-interest 98
Simon, R. 81
Singh, Basil 72
skills

for effective citizenship 36–7
    exercise of 114-15
    key skills approach 137–8
Smith, Jackie 67
social responsibility 9, 12–13
    resources for 107–9
social systems and structures 31
South Africa 18
Standards Fund 66
Stenhouse, Lawrence 72
Steutel, J. 13
summative assessment 129, 131-2
Swann, Frederick 6

Teacher Training Agency 66, 67
Teaching Citizenship journal 66
teaching and learning in citizenship 70–84
    critical faculties development 80–1
    strategies for teaching citizenship 73–80
    theoretical background 71–3
    training of teachers 60, 66–8
technology
    craft and design and 26
    information and communication and (ICT) 27,
        43
This is History 111
time issues 45, 48
Tooley, J. 88
Toolkit for School Councils 66
Towards Citizenship support pack 106
Trafford, B. 22
training of teachers 60, 66–8
transactional methods 47
Tudor, R. 101
Turner, Adam Newman 61

Ulster, University of 58
Understand the Law resource 107
Understanding Citizenship course 105
United Nations 113
    UN Children's Fund (UNICEF) 98
Uppsala, University of 58

Values Education Council 58
vocational education 25–6
Voiels, V. 89

Wales
    citizenship education in 16
    Welsh Assembly 112
Working Party for Citizenship Education 16, 56–7,
    66–9
worksheets 114, 115

Young, M. 87
Young Citizen's Passport 107
Young People's Passport 66
Youth Parliament Competition 60